THE CORPORATE LOOKING GLASS

Using Culture for Your Competitive Advantage

Rossina Gil

D1365274

ISBN 978-0-557-38051-0

*This book is dedicated in loving memory to
my mother, María Antonia Ruíz Mesa de Seville,
to whom I am forever indebted for instilling in me
faith, the spirit of adventure, hard work, and compassion.*

CONTENTS

INTRODUCTION

Relationships are the key to success in global business and in your personal life. At the heart of effective relationships are emotional skills. Some people are more developed in their emotional skills than others. To succeed in this diverse and fast-changing world, one must learn to become emotionally resilient. We gain resilience with perspective.

After more than ten years of practice as an executive coach for high-potentials and virtual teams for multi-national organizations, I have collected so many stories that I was once asked, "Is that story really true?" My response was, "Why wouldn't it be true?" The answer was, "Because you seem to have a story for everything!"

That is the crux of this book. Before literature and literacy, we had (and still have) storytelling. Add to this a dose of theory, and we have a way to balance the emotions that may resonate from the stories with the logic that dictates from Behavioral Science.

The objective of this book is to help alleviate some of the frustrations that stem from misunderstandings and idiosyncratic behavior in both the corporate world and life in general.

Other books similar to this theme of adaptation tend to offer a more narrow scope. This book examines successful human behavior from a holistic perspective...one that was acquired by more than a decade's worth of international executives sharing their scenarios, perspectives, and experiences with me. Think of it as a 360-degree review on Life. I share this with you, although names and corporate organizations have been changed or are kept anonymous for confidentiality purposes.

Please be advised that the information is no holds-barred. Some readers may be offended at the information shared. It is information which can help us learn and grow. As an American[1], I hope all visitors feel comfortable in expressing their Freedom of Speech; and, I always tell my clients that much like we would not care to have someone enter our physical home and disrespect us, we cannot visit another country and disrespect them with our unsolicited candor.

After reading this book, I hope you gain some insight as to how to make a more effective impact engaging with others and to gain some solace from understanding behavior of differing styles to your own.

Bear in mind, much like the author John Grisham, I do not proclaim to be the best writer AND I have something worthy to contribute.

Enjoy,

Rossina

---

[1] When I use the term "American," I am referring to citizens of the United States of America. Nationals from North, Central, and South America also consider themselves Americans.

CHAPTER 1

UNDERSTANDING "CULTURE"

"To know others is learned, to know yourself is wise."
– Lao Tzu, father of Taoism

What is culture? **Culture** is the way we make sense of the world and how we view it. It is the way one chooses to think and to behave. It is learned behavior. It is the software in your hardware. For many, culture really boils down to "the way things are done around here." Ed Schein, a respected figure in the field of Organization Development, describes culture as "artifacts, espoused values, and assumptions."

From our values, we develop a perspective from which we choose to view the world. This is our paradigm – how we see things. Perception is reality; and, sometimes that perception is distorted by our values and we see things differently. As a result, *we often see what we want to see*; not what exists and/or not what *else* exists. We also don't see what we don't expect to see. This is known as scotoma. **Scotoma** is when the mind blocks out the incongruity of the situation. Details that are there before our eyes are overridden. Take a look at this sketching:

What do you see?

While this is originated as "My Wife & My Mother-in-law;" most people say they see a young woman and/or an old woman…or, some say "hag" or "witch." Sometimes it is even hard to see the first picture after you have found the second. The young lady's body is facing your left and looking over her right shoulder away from you. The elderly lady is also facing your left and has a protruding, elongated chin that is resting down on her chest, and an oversized nose with a wart. The ear of the young lady is the eye of the elderly lady. The choker necklace of the young lady is the gaping mouth of the elderly lady.

What does this picture mean? Sometimes we look at a situation and we stop looking for the bigger picture because we think we know what is going on. There is no need to look further. We know, for example, that our regional office just "lied" about how well the process is going. We don't always stop to consider that maybe it wasn't a "lie," or that calling it a "lie" to their faces would damage the business relationship intra-company!

In new relationships, sometimes we search for what we desire to see and avoid the red flags that pop up left and right; or, the warnings that friends and family try to provide. Perhaps it is a shared perspective of what is considered gauche or tacky by one person (i.e. the old lady) is considered exciting or beautiful by another (i.e. the young lady). Take, for example, the following picture:

Here is a picture of a family of four visiting the United States from Colombia. They chose to dine at Hooters, a restaurant known for its buxom waitresses. In the USA, most parents would not take their teens and tweens (i.e. pre-teens) to a restaurant that boasts so much sexuality. Hooters is not known as being a family-fun dining spot, for Americans. Perhaps IHOP (a.k.a. International House of Pancakes), Island's, or Denny's might be an equivalent for a family desiring table service and a fast-food menu. However, Colombia is a rival to Venezuela, et al, in beauty pageants. Bikini-clad women adorn many calendars and offices throughout these regions. *Piropos*, translated as "flattery" or "compliments" (received by most American women as wolf whistles and sexual harassment) brighten a Colombian woman's day that she "still has it going on."

The bottom line with culture is there is no superior culture or inferior culture. There is no right or wrong behavior.[2] Typically the dominant culture attempts to obliterate the less influential culture. This may be attempted either directly or indirectly. For example, the British conquered Northern Ireland and enforced English on the Irish.

---

[2] This is not to say that violence, murder, or genocide is acceptable.

This is clearly a direct attempt at cultural dominance. The Irish have their Gaelic language. They make sure that the language is not lost among the younger generations. They fear cultural imperialism. **Cultural imperialism** is when a dominant culture attempts to impose its style on another culture and it usually perceives itself to be superior. An example of indirect cultural imperialism is the presence of McDonald's in France. French activist José Bové vandalized McDonald's in France. He protested against people changing their diets from French food to, his perception, grotesque food. Indeed, with the proliferation of fast-food restaurants, Japan is having its first generation of obese children. Is it *caveat emptor* (buyer beware) or *caveat venditor* (seller beware)?

Assimilation, by contrast, is when the less dominant group mimics cultural traits or behaviors of the dominant or more influential members of a particular culture. Despite women being in the slight majority in population in the USA, for example, many executive women attempt to assimilate into the male-dominated workforce – consciously or subconsciously. At one Fortune 100 company, one woman said she felt she "had" to cut her hair. She had luscious long locks, but felt the short bob was "more professional." Also, at an American *maquiladora*[3], Mexican women were pinning their hair up in buns. The men wanted to know why their female colleagues wouldn't literally let their hair down for work, and during a break I privately addressed this issue with the women. The answer was the same: it is "more professional." I've had female executives also refrain from wearing skirts because they felt it was "too feminine" – by which they meant "not corporate."

---

[3] A maquiladora, or maquila, is a manufacturing facility that is typically owned by an American company in Mexico.

IDENTITY IS DESTINY

We must be aware of what image we project because it affects how effective or successful we will be in reaching any objective, whether it be business, personal, or survival. Misunderstandings breed distrust. Distrust will not get us where we'd like to go. Indeed, there are those who love Americans and there are those who hate Americans, so your reputation as an American may precede you and there is only so much you can do about it. Once you are aware of how others perceive you, you have some material to work with; otherwise, you might fall into the same "box" as others from your background. Consider this article from the Sydney Morning Herald:

A quiet word to loud Americans[4] (sic)

LOUD and brash, in gawdy garb and baseball caps, shuffling between tourist sites or preparing to negotiate a business deal, they bemoan the failings of the world outside the United States.

The reputation of the ugly American abroad is not just some cruel stereotype. Rather, says the United States Government, it is worryingly accurate.

Now the State Department in Washington has joined forces with US industry to plan an image makeover by issuing guides on how to behave for Americans travelling overseas.

Under a program starting next month, several big US companies will give employees going abroad a "world citizen's guide" featuring 16 etiquette tips on how they can help improve their country's battered international image.

Business for Diplomatic Action, a non-profit group funded by large US companies, has met State Department officials to discuss

---

[4] Source: Philip Sherwell, Smh.com.au, April 17, 2006

issuing the guide with every newly issued American passport. The guide offers a series of "simple suggestions" under the slogan, "Help your country while you travel for your company."

The guide advises Americans to not just talk but to listen; to discuss and argue but not to be didactic, and not to foist a US world view on others.

The head of Business for Diplomatic Action, Keith Reinhard, said: "Surveys consistently show that Americans are viewed as arrogant, insensitive, over-materialistic and ignorant about local values. That, in short, is the image of the ugly American abroad and we want to change it."

The guide also offers tips on the dangers of dressing too casually, and the pluses of learning a few words of the local language, using hand gestures[5] and even map reading. Business for Diplomatic Action has distributed 200,000 passport-sized guides tailored to students.

RED ALERTS FOR TRAVEL

From the guidelines:

Think as big as you like but talk and act smaller. In many countries, any form of boasting is considered very rude. Talking about wealth, power or status - corporate or personal - can create resentment.

Listen at least as much as you talk. By all means, talk about America and your life in our country. But also ask people you're visiting about themselves and their way of life.

---

[5] Of course, where were the cultural advisors for President H.W. Bush when he stepped off of Air Force One in Australia flashing the inverted "V" for Victory hand sign, which is "F-you" in Australia? The palm must face out to represent "V" for Victory.

Save the lectures for your kids. Whatever your subject of discussion, let it be a discussion not a lecture. Justified or not, the US is seen as imposing its will on the world.

Think a little locally. Try to find a few topics that are important in the local popular culture. Remember, most people in the world have little or no interest in the World Series or the Super Bowl. What we call "soccer" is called "football" everywhere else. And it's the most popular sport on the planet.

Slow down. We talk fast, eat fast, move fast, live fast. Many cultures do not.

Speak lower and slower. A loud voice is often perceived as bragging. A fast talker can be seen as aggressive.

Your religion is your religion and not necessarily theirs. Religion is usually considered deeply personal, not a subject for public discussions.

If you talk politics, talk - don't argue. Steer clear of arguments about American politics, even if someone is attacking US politicians or policies. Agree to disagree.

<u>Australian Preparing to Repatriate:</u>

"I have grown used to certain Americanisms - talking loudly, being more direct & demanding, and some of it may have rubbed off on me (which is a good thing!). I will have to make a conscious effort when back in Oz to change some of my language, to say *mobile phone* (not cellphone) and *rubbish* (not trash), etc, or my Australian colleagues will not let me hear the end of it!"

MAIN STREET USA

What is the dominant, mainstream culture of the USA? We call it the WASP (White Anglo-Saxon Protestant) male. The **mainstream** culture is the culture that exerts the most influence over the regional occupants. Some people might think that to say both "White" and "Anglo-Saxon" is redundant; however, that is to distinguish from other "Whites" or Caucasians, e.g. Iranians. If a person is WASP female, then she is part of the sub-culture, by virtue of her gender creating a different set of circumstances (both biological and environmental). Indeed, a woman and a man from the same country speaking together is considered a cross-cultural dialogue.

German to USA:

> "I can speak better with any man in the whole world than my own German wife!"

Sub-cultures are all of the other cultures that exist in the region of the mainstream culture. They co-exist on various, selected levels. Aside from gender, racial, and religious sub-cultures, we have other biological, socio-cultural, and selected sub-cultures as well – such as, generational, socio-economic, and educational. Right now a major issue for corporations is recruiting and retaining talent from the Millennial group, which are those young people in the workforce, born 1981 or after.

> "Children today are tyrants. They contradict their parents, gobble their food, and tyrannize their teachers." - Socrates (470-399 B.C.)

Here is a breakdown of the current **four main generational groups**:

1. **Traditionalist** (born 1901 – 1945)

    - 75 million members
    - Also known as (a.k.a): Veterans, Silent Generation, GI's, Seniors, WWII Generation, Matures

2. **Boomer** (born 1946 – 1964)

   - 80 Million members

   - a.k.a: Baby Boomers

3. **Generation X** (born 1965 – 1980)

   - 46 million members

   - a.k.a: Xers, Baby Busters, Post-Boomers

4. **Millennial** (1981 – 1999)

   - 76 million members

   - a.k.a: Nexters, Generation Y, Echo Boom, Baby Busters, Boomerang, Generation Next, Internet Generation, Generation Net, Nintendo Generation

Again, those who are not considered part of the mainstream group are typically criticized by the dominant group. For example: "Younger employees are less *committed* because they are not working the hours that older employees are." Senior Management tends to be in the older age group. And, despite having a law that upholds 40 hours weekly as being full-time, the expectation is for employees to work more hours. I had one British woman remark: "I discovered if you give someone your cell phone number, they will call you (after hours)!"

The above statement of "less committed" implicates the value judgment that the younger group is not as good as the older group. It also makes the assumption that the groups operate differently due to generational differences. How can we re-phrase the observation with more objectivity and less inherent bias?

Answer: What are the differences in hours worked on the job? And, as a follow-up question we then ask: Are these generation-based differences? Research conducted by Administaff found that the number of hours worked in a week is <u>not</u> related to:

- Generation
- Race
- Country of origin

Number of hours worked in a week <u>is</u> related to:

- **Level in the company** - Employees at the top of the organization work longer hours than employees lower in the company hierarchy.

- **Type of employer** - Employees who work for for-profit organizations work more hours on average than employees who work for non-profit organizations.

- **Having children** - Employees who have children work fewer hours.

What is really happening is that we all have a tendency to view ourselves as consisting as part of the norm. I once asked an American client, "Why did you write your age as 34.5?" Her answer? "Everybody does that." Sure, everyone does that...under age 10! What was apparent to me is that she is precise and detailed. Culture is relative to our own viewpoint. While the Swiss say we Americans have excellent customer service, the Japanese say our customer service is extremely poor. The British think we're very friendly, and the Brazilians think we're as cold as frogs. Who is correct? They all are! *It all depends on your POV* (Point of View). What are the implications? This doesn't make you wrong...the feedback (a gift) makes you aware of how you can adapt, *if you want to win*. Let them think they're right all they wish, you're in it to win.

Remember, comments you make in regards to others reflect back as to who you are and what your expectations are. Take your hand and point at an object...The French have a saying, when you point at someone, there are three fingers pointing back at you.

So, if someone says, for example, that you talk too much, the three fingers could be:

1) Does s/he not talk enough?

2) Does s/he want more attention?

3) Does s/he not know how to interject?

The main points here are, *there is nothing wrong with your style* AND *it requires some adjusting for that particular person and/or group.*

CHAPTER 2

TYPES OF CULTURE

"What is necessary to change a person is to change his awareness of himself." – Abraham Maslow

I cover three types of culture: national, individual, and corporate. If you've moved from your corporate office in downtown over to the Westside, or from rural to urban, or from domestic to international, you may have noticed that the "rules" – rather, the *process* -- have changed. Analogous to this experience is the character Alice, of Alice in Wonderland, where she knows how to play croquet, but finds many aspects of the game have changed.

NATIONAL CULTURE

National, or regional, cultural differences can be equally as dramatic. Much like understanding the corporate culture, the change of environment may directly impact the way people choose to work. Take, for example, the French executive who is accustomed to spending three hours over lunch. France has the leading gastronomic region of the world in Lyon, so there are not many French who feel that the mid-day meal should be "rushed."[6] Such an executive would not understand the haste to get back to the office.

---

[6] Of course, there are other reasons such tradition and relationship or process-orientation, as well, to spending more time than the 30-60 minute lunch.

New Zealander to California:

"Everything is BIG: You can buy 72 packets of M&Ms or 32 rolls of toilet paper as one item. I counted 17 different types of milk.

Food: Far too many choices for everything, e.g. aisles of sugar-laden cereal. Cooking for 1 is bizarre - can normally get 2 meals out of an American size portion though!

Housing: Light switches are upside down.

Driving: Freeways can be 7 lanes in one direction and have maniac drivers. Driving on the wrong side of the road is not that bad (once you get in the right door).

Entertainment: 250+ channels on cable TV and nothing on - but there is a whole channel for tennis or reggae music. 3D ads on TV during the Super Bowl (American football) - dawky glasses required and all.

General stuff: It's possible to wear shorts in winter in California - 27 deg (80F) is hardly winter!! Voice recognition phone systems can't understand the Kiwi accent – 'yes' is difficult to understand apparently. It's 'gas' not fuel, 'trash' not rubbish, 'candy' not lollies, 'cookies' not biscuits. Couldn't be sure there weren't aliens from 'Men in Black' in the US Postal Service office.

Work stuff: Lots of security including padlocks on laptops, and guards whose sole purpose seems to be to wave all day."

INDIVIDUAL CULTURE

Individual culture is who you are as a person, and how you differ or relate to those from your national culture, or sub-culture. Whether it is by personality or life experience, you have a *preferred* way of doing things.

What is essential to your success in dealing with others from diversified backgrounds is your level of comfort with equifinality. **Equifinality** is the concept that there is not just one way to achieve your goals. Is it possible for you to meet your objective(s) by taking an alternative approach or methodology? Or, is the issue more about your personal need for control? As Socrates said millennia ago, "The only thing that is constant is change." He further observed: adapt or fail – which is essentially what Charles Darwin also deduced: evolve or die.

SELF-ASSESSMENT TOOLS

There are many Behavorial Science application tools that have been created to measure and define your individual culture and your corporate culture. Given these results, a sociologist or cross-cultural expert can help you examine how much of a stretch you would have to make from your Natural Style (who you are at home) to the Adapted Style (how you show up for work). Bottom line is: the less of a stretch, the better. We look to see that the results overlap fairly nicely to reduce the amount of culture shock, which produces stress. **Culture Shock** is when expectations and the reality of the experience do not meet. Most people expect behavior to remain the same from place to place. For example, many Americans assume that because the British speak English[7] that "we are the same." It is this mentality that contributes to a relatively high failure rate for American expatriates in the United Kingdom to complete corporate objectives.

---

[7] The British refuse to concede that they speak the same language as Americans. Britons speak British English; Americans speak American English.

American to Dominican Republic:

"Thankfully, things are looking up and I can start to relax and just 'experience' the Dominican culture now. Perhaps I was threatened at first by being thrown into a new way of life and wondering how I was going to fit in. Now I realize I don't have to become a 'Dominican' to enjoy their culture. I can still be an 'American' and keep my identity and values that I've accumulated throughout my life. That knowledge has changed the entire experience for me. Some things just can't be taught out of a book - you just have to go through it yourself to understand it."

American to Japan:

"The working space here is also something to talk about. I have 1 meter left to right, and about 3/4 meter front to back for my desk. I share a table with 7 other people. Fortunately, I have my own phone. There is no voice mail here so everyone jumps for the phones. It drives me crazy! We are constantly interrupted by other people's phones because there are so many people in the same space that you can't just 'let voice mail handle it' like we do at home.

You MUST pick up the phone, and the sooner the better. So one problem about coming in early is that I'm usually the only one here, except for the 'big' boss. So I can't just let the phones ring. I have to answer them! That bugs me. The answer is always the same, 'Oh, they aren't there? OK, I'll call back.' The reason I like to come early is that I can get more work done because it gets so loud in here it is hard to concentrate because of the density of people. Sometimes I need to go to the library just to think. The other reason I come in early is so that I can leave at a reasonable time. As you know, the Japanese work very late. That's why they come in late. They know the pressure will be there to work late, so why come in early? I am always the first to leave. You might want to tell that to other American Expats. They may face the pressure of leaving first, be ready to stand up to it."

The following is a partial list of self-assessment tools that measure value preferences:

- **Ntrinsx.** This tool was developed by a process-oriented software engineer, Bob Hill, and a relationship-oriented Human Resources attorney, Lisa Yankowitz.   It is a synthesized, easier-to-retain version of the MBTI.

- **DISC (Dominance Influence Steadiness Compliance).** There are several types of DISC, which are more or less the same model based on four quadrants and can be utilized on individuals or teams. It was developed by John Geier, et al, and based on the work of psychologist William Moulton Marston, Michael Laudrup, Walter V. Clarke, and others.

- **Cultural Orientation Inventory (COI).** This was developed by Training Management Corporation (TMC), which was acquired by Berlitz Cross-Cultural Consulting. This tool can measure the individual's culture against specific cultures.

- **Strategic Alignment Survey (SAS).** Designed by Integro Leadership Institute, the SAS measures culture change specific to levels of alignment, trust and engagement.

- **Cross-Cultural Adaptability Inventory.** This was created by Colleen Kelley, PhD and Judith Meyers, PsyD. Their scales can be used in assessing candidates for multi-cultural organizations and for boundary spanning positions.

- **The International Profiler (TIP)**. This questionnaire and feedback process comes from WorldWork, based in London. It helps managers and professionals reflect on what their strengths and areas for improvement are in working internationally.

LEARNING STYLES

One McDonald's Corporation instructional method is the **four-step learning delivery**. This approach implements the strongest three learning styles into one simple process. First step, the instructor **TELLS (Auditory)** you how to do something (let's call it "X process") while you listen. Second step, the instructor **SHOWS (Visual)** you how to do the X process while you observe and s/he repeats the steps verbally during the demonstration. Third step, the instructor asks you to **TRY (Tactile/Kinesthetic)** to do the X process while you together repeat the steps verbally. Fourth step, the instructor asks you to **INSTRUCT** (cognitive recall) another individual on the X process. Much of learning is reinforced when you instruct others. And, note that repetition is key in learning new material.

It is helpful to understand what your preferred learning style is. Are you a Visual learner? An Auditory learner? Or, a Tactile/Kinesthetic learner? A quick test that I like to administer to help you determine which style you have is: Suppose that you haven't followed what it is I'm trying to communicate to you, and then I succeed in clarifying my point. How would you complete the following response to indicate that you have understood me? "I _____what you mean! I _____what you are saying!" If you said, "I *see* what you mean! I *see* what you are saying!" then you are visual. If you said, "I *hear* what you mean! I *hear* what you are saying!" then you are auditory. If you said, "I *have got a grasp of* what you mean! I *get* what you are saying!" chances are you are tactile/kinesthetic.

Here are clues to identifying a **visual** learner:
- Prefers visual aids (pictures, graphs).

- Prefers to see it (for example, a foreign word) in order to feel that they've grasped the material.

- May experience difficulty in recall or comprehension of spoken instructions or information.

How can you present information to a **visual** learner to make your information clear? You can accommodate a visual learner's preferred learning style by the following:

- Provide written directions, instructions, information.

- Enhance your presentation with relevant visual aids to stimulate memory recall.

- Offer them paper and markers for taking notes or for doodling. (NOTE: Many doodlers have been misperceived as lacking interest in a business meeting, when it helps them stay focused).

- Present demonstrations or employ role playing to illustrate the learning information.

Here are clues to identifying an **auditory** learner:

- Prefers to gain information by listening -- these are the types who can drive their cars and learn a foreign language by repeating the word(s) on the language learning CD.

- Prefers to hear it in order to understand.

- May experience difficulty following written directions (anything written) because the focus is more on tone and other nuances of language and sound.

How can you present information to an **auditory** leaner to make your information clear? You can accommodate an auditory learner's preferred learning style by the following:

- Provide spoken directions, instructions, information.

- Transfer knowledge by using verbal methods such as discussions, debates, and small groups.

- Employ learning activities that have learners repeat content.

Here are clues to identifying a tactile/kinesthetic learner:

- Prefers hands-on learning
- Prefers to do it to understand how to do it correctly.
- Feels most comfortable and learns best when s/he is involved in active, experiential activities.

How can you present information to a **tactile/kinesthetic** learner to make your information clear? You can accommodate a tactile/kinesthetic learner's preferred learning style by the following:

- Provide lots of physical learning activities.
- Take frequent breaks and/or invite any type of movement during the session.
- Employ technical learning, i.e. Wii, computer, etc. to reinforce material.

Facilitators can get a sense of what learning styles others have by gaining an understanding of how people work. For example, do you handle your work by speaking on the phone more than engaging directly with people? Do you prefer e-mail or site location visits? When a client does not comprehend the material, it is best to present the information by using a different learning style to make the information more clear.

Some learners are more Task-oriented and others are more Process-oriented. The **Task-oriented learners** are comfortable with trial and error. The focus is on *momentum and quantity*. As Americans, we have learned to "fall off the horse, and get back on it again." That is part of our Cowboy history. We came as Pilgrims who starved if they did not learn the rules of the New World. Task-oriented learners are happy to "brainstorm" (an American term) for ideas; implement one, and see how it works. If it doesn't work out, another solution will be implemented. Perhaps the end goal slightly changes along the way; but, eventually the objective is reached. These learners tend to be risk-takers. An example I always like to offer is that while Germany and Japan were world-renown for their engineering and robotics, it was the USA that led the world in taking risks that led to the success and establishment of Silicon Valley. The model might look like this following graph:

TASK-ORIENTATION

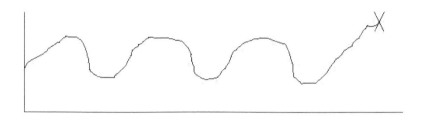

PROCESS-ORIENTATION

Process-oriented learners prefer to acquire a lot of knowledge before they begin implementation. The focus is on *quality*. These learners may demonstrate this preference from as early as the toddler stage. As toddlers, they may not speak any singular words and then one day open their mouths to utter a complete sentence. These are the adults who require endless meetings, data, information, and time to read materials before they feel comfortable with making a decision. These learners tend to be risk-averse. The model to illustrate the progress towards reaching the objective might look like the second graph above.

CHAPTER 3

UNDERSTANDING SELF - BEYOND VALUES

"The only thing we have to fear is fear itself."
— Franklin D. Roosevelt

To be most powerful in influencing others and for the purpose of self development, there is much to be gained in the goal of expanding your personal comfort zone as much as possible. Fear limits expansion of that comfort zone which, in turn, inhibits development. Fear creates associated needs to cope with that emotion. Your challenge is to face your behavior in four common areas and examine how they reduce your effectiveness. These four areas are known as the Four Fatal Fears.[8]

There is a lot of self-justification that is practiced in situations that trigger reactions from you, typically, because your experience has taught you that you need to protect yourself. It is an automatic, psychological survival mechanism. There is no sense in flaying yourself for your behavior. Rather, recognize where your past experience(s) may cause you to react in a way that is not reflected in the reactions of others when they are exposed to precisely the same scenario.

---

[8] Psychologist Maxie Maultsby's coined the term the "Four Fatal Fears."

FOUR FATAL FEARS

<u>Fear</u>: Fear of **Being Wrong** <u>Associated Need</u>: **Being Right** <u>How it shows up</u>: argumentative, arrogant <u>What you avoid</u>: where you could fail or make mistakes	<u>Fear</u>: Fear of **Losing** <u>Associated Need</u>: **Need to Win** <u>How it shows up</u>: tend to see things as win-lose <u>What you avoid</u>: situations where you could lose
<u>Fear</u>: Fear of **Rejection** <u>Associated Need</u>: **To Be Liked/Accepted** <u>How it shows up</u>: challenge, accommodating, ingratiating yourself to people, indirectness, white lies <u>What you avoid</u>: conflict, challenging the group, avoid people who are different, honesty	<u>Fear</u>: Fear of **Emotional Discomfort** <u>Associated Need</u>: **To Be in Control** <u>How it shows up</u>: stoicism, avoiding feelings of guilt, anger, intimacy, sharing embarrassment, stonewalling, blame <u>What you avoid</u>: situations where authenticity is needed, all emotional situations, conflict

Have you noticed any patterns in your life as they relate to these four fears? Another way to describe this hypothesis is what I call the **Kicked Puppy Syndrome**. This syndrome is when someone projects their anger onto you, it is really a reaction to a trigger that has its origin in the past. *It is not you.* It is, however, what you represent.

I coined the term Kicked Puppy Syndrome from a personal story of being bitten by a dog that had been kicked when it was a puppy. One day, I was walking my bike up a steep driveway that was shared by my friend and her neighbor. The neighbor's two dogs came out barking as I passed by. They were unleashed. One of them casually walked over and around my bike to me and bit me on the thigh. I had done nothing to antagonize the dog, and it felt aggression. After my friend spoke with her neighbor, the neighbor informed us that his dog had been kicked as a puppy by someone on a bicycle. It was re-living a script because, unbeknownst to me, my sheer presence (in an undesirable context of having a bike) had caused it to experience this specific insecurity.

What pain are you carrying forward from your past that is affecting your interactions with others in your present experience? Can you identify any situations which make you angry yet don't make others around you equally as angry? Think back to the last person who made you angry...Is it something similar to what someone in your past did to you? Did that person disrespect you in a way, which left you feeling dumb (Fear of Being Wrong)? Unwanted (Fear of Being Rejected)? A failure (Fear of Losing)? Uncomfortable (Fear of Emotional Discomfort)? Embrace the chaos and learn from the lessons within the mayhem. This is your opportunity for growth.

JOHARI WINDOW

One way to examine our interpersonal communication and relationships is with the Johari Window. The Johari Window is a cognitive psychological tool developed by Joseph Luft and Harry Ingham. It is exemplified much like window panes connected with four intersecting quadrants.

	Known by Others	Unknown by Others
Known to Self	Open window	Hidden window
Unknown to Self	Blind Spot window	Mystery window

The **Open** window is what is known by others and what you know about yourself. This is what you are willing to share with others. Examples could be information you disclose in a bio or Facebook.

The **Hidden** window is what is <u>not</u> known by others, yet what you know about yourself. This is what you are consciously and deliberately trying to hide from others. Examples include relationships, habits, the past, prejudices, etc. Self-disclosure decreases the size of the Hidden window and increases the size of the Open window. This can result in improved interpersonal relationships because often the vulnerability you expose grants the perception that you are human. The more authentic you are with others in disclosing your whole self, the more likely they are to trust you, understand you, and value your relationship. Organizationally, off-site retreats are often designed to broaden this window. It takes risk to open and build trust with others, and many fear that the disclosure will backfire as judgment and/or a misperception of weakness. This is always a risk.

The **Blind Spot** window is what is known by others, yet <u>not</u> known to you about yourself. These are messages we unconsciously hide from ourselves, yet they are communicated to others. We learn about these pieces of information when someone offers the "gift" of feedback (however, well or poorly wrapped). This window is expanded organizationally through the usage of 360's, 1:1's (i.e. one-on-one's), and coaching. Receiving feedback can help you move from a Blind Spot window to an Open window.

The **Mystery (Unknown)** window is what is <u>not</u> known by others and what is <u>not</u> known by you about yourself. These are things in our unconscious that we conceal from ourselves. This concealment is often for a reason: we aren't ready to accept them, and we are not ready to change, so we don't think about them. This information is often surfaced through counseling, group therapy, or dreams. Examples include a desire for adventure, release of sublimated emotions that contribute to addictions and/or other fears, discovering your purpose in life, "hidden talents," etc.

Any data that moves from the Blind Spot or Mystery (i.e. Unknown to Self) windows into your Open or Hidden (i.e. Known to Self) windows would indicate increased self-knowledge – or personal growth. That information makes those window panes larger, which is the goal for personal and professional growth. **Building self-awareness is the No. 1 skill for improving your Emotional Intelligence (EQ).** EQ is at the heart of cultivating relationships. Since, business is relationships, let's examine EQ.

Emotion is different from feeling because it represents a psycho-physiological state that moves an organism to action. According to Dr. Paul Ekman, there are seven universal emotions. They are the following: **Contempt, Disgust, Anger, Sadness, Surprise, Fear, and Joy**. These emotions are called universal because he found that the expressions for these emotions are innate and are therefore understood regardless of one's cultural origin. To test his theory, he brought pictures of these authentic emotions to a remote village in Papua, New Guinea – a place where the civilization was left untouched by the outside world and could not have learned these expressions.

What is important to bear in mind is that while emotional expression is universal, emotional triggers vary by individual and culture, and *"scripts from the past"* can affect their intensity. **Scripts** are imported when people have feelings that have been left unresolved. Most likely it is because you were too young when something happened that placed you in a position where your feelings were never fully or satisfactorily expressed, or, perhaps, did not lead to the outcome you desired. These scripts from the past are what I refer to as your Kicked Puppy Syndrome. As a reminder, the **Kicked Puppy Syndrome** is when your present reality is distorted by your script and causes inappropriate emotional reactions.

What was it that happened in your past that *really* gets under your skin today? You feel that you are being dominated. How do you react? Or, do you *not* react by stonewalling? If you stonewall, that is an emotional signal that indicates you feel overpowered and are feeling unable or are unwilling to deal with the matter. From the research that Dr. Ekman conducted, he concluded that these acquired emotional triggers create new pathways in the brain….Pathways that don't necessarily exist in others around us who have not suffered the same experience. In essence, you have been re-programmed.

To feel emotion is to be human, so we don't necessarily want to turn them off. What we do want to learn in order to be most effective is to develop the habit of *"attentiveness"* (similar to *mindfulness*). We need to learn to cool our hot emotional triggers and avoid destructive emotional episodes.

A better understanding of what drives our reactions gives us the opportunity to make less emotional, more reasoned choices about our judgments and our ensuing behavior. Better interpersonal relationships may result from behavior stemming from choice rather than emotional reactions. How many times have we said things from impulse, without thinking, and have regretted it? Behaving from choice allows for more consideration. This is one reason why the Japanese have the proverb: *Silence is Golden. Speech is Silver.*

How much thought is given towards what is shared? Are you speaking for the sake of being heard? For the sake of being recognized? For the sake of your Need to be Accepted? Or, from the discomfort of silence?

Why is it important for us to understand ourselves and our emotional triggers?

- **Personal Awareness**. If you are aware of your biases and how a particular environment can affect you, you can direct a system in the direction you would like to go instead of being carried away.

- **Other Awareness**.   Just by showing up, you are an intervention. You may not have opened your mouth, but someone else's script might have been activated by just the very look of you or their awareness of your title. This, in turn, alters their environment.

CHAPTER 4

ORGANIZATIONAL CULTURE

Organizational Culture is a pattern of assumptions, values, and norms which are shared by organization members. **Norms** are unwritten rules of behavior that guide what members of groups do and don't do. Norms serve a need, such as group cohesion, and provide predictability. Predictability keeps most members feeling safe because they learn the nature of the "reward band." A **reward band** is recognition, bonuses, promotion, favoritism, extended to those who behave accordingly.

However, norms are mostly unconscious and might not reflect actual written policies. They may also be contrary to whatever values the organization espouses to hold. This is why it is paramount that new members identify the norms as early as possible in order to avoid pitfalls and land mines.

Here is one example of a norm I observed at a women's conference...on the first day, the employees were given a stylish, organic cotton long-sleeved top with a Chinese emblem on the front. For many companies, the employees might interpret that gift as a symbol of unity or team membership and would have worn it on the second day. This organization, however, had a norm that the employees wear professional wear for all work-related functions. It did not have to be written down in a formal policy for employees to know that that is *not* something they should do. Naturally, one of the newer employees was the sole person to show up wearing the shirt.

On the other hand, there is a company in France which did create a formal policy that no white socks are to be worn to work. This policy was created on the perception that many American men choose to wear white socks with their trousers and dress shoes, which the French find to be distasteful and distracting.   Policies, written or unwritten, define expectations of group norms.

A Norms Assessment can help determine readiness for change. Mapping the norms can help an organization create an effective strategy. The focus would be on the pivotal norms versus peripheral norms.

Pivotal norms are those that the group pinpoints as critical to its survival. Given such importance, they are harder to change. Violators of this norm suffer strong consequences.

Peripheral norms are easier to change because of their lower intensity. As they are of less importance to the group, they are thus easier to violate. Violators do not usually suffer strong consequences.

To identify a pivotal norm for a mapping process, we need to follow four steps:

1. **Identify the Norm**. "Around here, when it comes to ___(behavior)___ we ___(action)___."

   E.g. Around here, when it comes to "feedback," we "handle it face-to-face discreetly" or "handle it in the hallway with a colleague" or "take it straight to Human Resources (HR)," etc.

   Around here, when it comes to "working weekends," we "regularly come in on Saturdays," or "can work from home" or "have this reduced to just travel," etc.

   Around here, when it comes to "vacation/Paid Time Off (PTO)" we "are contactable by cell only for emergencies," or "are not contactable" or "are always contactable," etc.

2. **Diagnose the Norm**: How is it encouraged, supported, discouraged?

3. **Impact:** Is the impact positive, neutral, or negative?

4. Frequency: Is the frequency frequent, infrequent, or neither?

Culture can evolve intentionally and unintentionally. By understanding a culture's norms, we can work towards the desired outcome. This applies to understanding family cultures (the in-laws), national cultures (expats), and corporate cultures (employees).

Leadership can be provided by any person who is an influencer. While lower-levels of management can certainly instill a culture from the ground up, the trickle-down effect of Senior Management has the highest potential for the quickest results. Ed Schein argues that culture is created by what those leaders pay attention to, measure, and control. Employees learn how to behave from their understanding of how leaders react to critical incidents and crises.[9] Leaders' deliberate role modeling results in mimicry.[10] Culture among employees evolves in the direction that is set by leaders in how they allocate resources and rewards. This includes recruitment, promotions, retirements, and the excommunication of members.

The **sustained competitive advantage** is attained if the organization is valuable, rare, and imperfectly inimitable. Take, for example, Southwest Airlines. It has sustained a competitive advantage over all airlines for over 20 years. No other airline has even come close to matching that record. When other airlines request an opportunity to conduct first-hand research into the Southwest Way, they are welcomed with open arms because Southwest management has strong confidence that they are inimitable. Two core values to its success are Collectivism (i.e. team spirit) and Egalitarianism (i.e. pilots are not superior). By fully understanding the impact of the positive attributes of its culture and the effects of the negative attributes, a competing airline/organization can create an organizational strategy

---

[9] The Chinese have two characters to represent the word crisis. They are "chaos" and "opportunity."

[10] Toddlers often practice mimicry after their parents.

that rivals Southwest (such as the former Southwest employees who went on to create the fierce rival JetBlue).

Cameron & Quinn offer what they call the **Competing Values Model.**[11] In this model, power resides in the integration approach of the four major culture types: Clan, Hierarchy, Market, Adhocracy. The two dimensions are: flexibility/discretion versus stability/control and internal focus and integration versus external focus and differentiation.

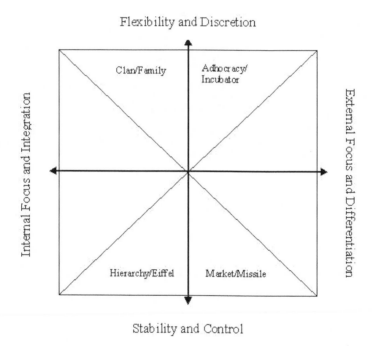

Flexibility and Discretion

Clan/Family   Adhocracy/Incubator

Internal Focus and Integration   External Focus and Differentiation

Hierarchy/Eiffel   Market/Missile

Stability and Control

---

[11] Cameron, Kim S.; Quinn, Robert E. <u>Diagnosing and Changing Organizational Culture</u>. Jossey-Bass:San Francisco. 2006. pg. 46.

The CLAN / FAMILY culture

- An organization that focuses on internal maintenance with flexibility, concern for people, and sensitivity to customers.

Relationships between Employees	Diffuse relationships to organic whole to which one is bonded
Attitude toward Authority	Status is ascribed to parent figures who are close and powerful
Ways of Thinking and Learning	Intuitive, holistic, lateral, and error-correcting
Attitudes toward People	Family members
Ways of Changing	"Parent" changes course
Ways of Motivating and Rewarding	Intrinsic satisfaction in being loved and respected
Management Style	Management by subjectives
Criticism and Conflict Resolution	Turn other cheek, save others' faces, do not lose power game

The HIERARCHY / EIFFEL TOWER culture

- An organization that focuses on internal maintenance with a need for stability and control.

Relationships between Employees	Specific role in mechanical system of required interactions
Attitude toward Authority	Status is ascribed to superior roles, which are distant yet powerful
Ways of Thinking and Learning	Logical, analytical, vertical and rationally efficient
Attitudes toward People	Human Resources
Ways of Changing	Change rules and procedures
Ways of Motivating and Rewarding	Promotion to greater position, larger role
Management Style	Management by job description
Criticism and Conflict Resolution	Criticism is accusation of irrationalism unless there are procedures to arbitrate conflicts

The MARKET / GUIDED MISSILE culture

- An organization that focuses on external positioning with a need for stability and control.

Relationships between Employees	Specific tasks in cybernetic system targeted upon shared objectives
Attitude toward Authority	Status is achieved by project group members who contribute to targeted goal
Ways of Thinking and Learning	Problem centered, professional, practical, cross-disciplinary
Attitudes toward People	Specialists and experts
Ways of Changing	Shift aim as target moves
Ways of Motivating and Rewarding	Pay or credit for performance and problems solved
Management Style	Management by objectives
Criticism and Conflict Resolution	Constructive task-related only, then admit error fast and correct

The ADHOCRACRY / INCUBATOR culture

- An organization that focuses on external positioning with a high degree of flexibility and individuality.

Relationships between Employees	Diffuse, spontaneous relationship growing out of shared creative process
Attitude toward Authority	Status is achieved by individuals exemplifying creativity and growth
Ways of Thinking and Learning	Process-oriented, creative, ad hoc, inspirational
Attitudes toward People	Co-creators
Ways of Changing	Improvise and attune
Ways of Motivating and Rewarding	Participating in the process of creating new realities
Management Style	Management by enthusiasm
Criticism and Conflict Resolution	Must improve creative idea, not negate it

A new culture can evolve from the understanding of the manifestations of its values, beliefs, and assumptions. Once successful organizations, such as Sears Roebuck & Co., have declined or vanished. How can you and/or your organization avoid similar fate?

There are two main questions to ask when creating a success strategy:

(1)   How do we survive as entity?

(2)   How do we maintain our survival?

SAMPLE APPROACHES FOR DESIGNING A SUCCESS STRATEGY

Culture is tied to people's organization success. Why? There is power/emotion in culture. It pushes people to behavior accordingly, even when the best results are not being produced. Therefore, your culture needs to match your strategy to be successful.

Appreciative Inquiry is the idea that the organization is a miracle to be embraced rather than a problem to be solved. **Focus is placed on what works, rather than trying to fix what doesn't.** While its origins are from early action research theorists, it was further developed and popularized by David Cooperrider and Suresh Srivatsva in the 1980's. By asking questions that are appreciative, applicable, provocative, and collaborative, positive relationships are built. The traditional approach to change is: What problems are you having? The focus of Appreciative Inquiry is on the contribution of individuals who, together, establish trust and organizational alignment. It is the parts that make the whole. It is about accountability. *What are you willing to do* to make the situation be a winning one? – Not about who is right. It is turning away from the mentality of "Not in My Back Yard" (**NIMBY**).

The following five steps are the 5D-model for Appreciative Inquiry:

1. **DEFINE**: Select the areas of inquiry and learning.

2. **DISCOVER:** Identify what gives life to an organization. What happens when an organization is at its best? What is working around here? Appreciate the best of what is working.

3. **DREAM:** Envision processes that would work well in the future. What do we want the organization to become? Dialogue about "what could be."

4. **DESIGN:** Create processes that create the ideal. Innovate "what will be."

5. **DELIVER:** Execute the proposed design.

You need alignment for Strategic Change. Once an organization realizes its core identity and qualities and has designed a clear vision statement, an infrastructure can be created into which business processes are developed. This way, organizations can achieve consistency and synergy through the realization of its core qualities.

Conventionally, **organizational architecture** consists of the following five areas:

1. **Strategy** – Vision, governance, comparative advantage

2. **Structure** – Power & authority, information flow, organizational roles

3. **Process** – Networks, process teams, integrative roles, matrix structures

4. **Reward Systems** – Compensation & rewards

5. **People/HR Management** – Hiring, work feedback, learning

There are various models used to assess how changing one area can lead to impacting others. Jay Galbraith's Five-Star Model is one such model that is used as a visual to create alignment. The quotations alongside the starpoint modules are added to provide further clarification.[12]

---

[12] Source: Courtesy of Pepperdine MSOD program

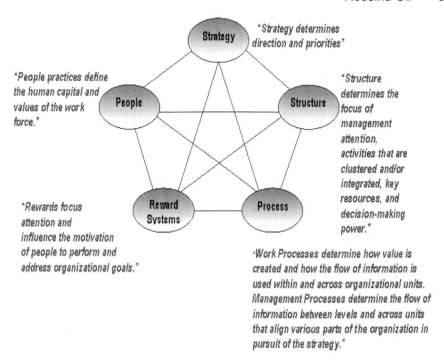

"Strategy determines direction and priorities"

"People practices define the human capital and values of the work force."

"Structure determines the focus of management attention, activities that are clustered and/or integrated, key resources, and decision-making power."

"Rewards focus attention and influence the motivation of people to perform and address organizational goals."

"Work Processes determine how value is created and how the flow of information is used within and across organizational units. Management Processes determine the flow of information between levels and across units that align various parts of the organization in pursuit of the strategy."

CHAPTER 5

THE CULTURAL ADJUSTMENT CURVE

<u>American to Qatar:</u>

"Every time I begin to get comfortable I seem to have a Dorothy (Wizard of Oz) experience, 'We're not in Kansas anymore.' "

Even though many people refer to the term Change Management as synonymous with Organization Development, it is important to make distinctions between the words "change" and "transition."

Change is external and situational. For example, starting a new position begins on your first day of employment. Changes deal with any type of restructuring of an organization. It happens when anything begins or ends in our lives.

Transition is internal, and often emotional. It is the psychological process we go through in order to come to terms with a new situation. Therefore, it takes longer than change. You may have taken on a new assignment (change); the adaptation to the new role (transition) is a longer process. People must psychologically fully embrace the change in order to work at the most productive levels; otherwise, there is discomfort.

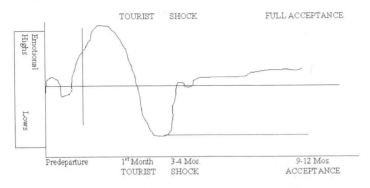

Let's examine the Cultural Adjustment Curve as an example of transition. Prior to the start of an assignment (or a new role), you are in the Pre-Departure phase. In **Pre-Departure** stage, there may be a mixture of up's and down's emotionally. People generally feel excited at another opportunity presented to them, as well as the stresses involved in making a change, e.g. letting go of colleagues, families, selling/leasing the house/apartment – essentially anything that is familiar and comforting.

The vertical line represents the start of your next phase in life. You have arrived. The rising excitement prior to your arrival suddenly catapults to a high. This is called the Tourist, or Honeymoon, period. This stage typically lasts for a month. In the **Tourist** stage, you are searching for things that appeal to you. You want to see the desirable aspects of your new assignments. What I refer to as a "positive red flag" is when people at this stage start to positively stereotype the behavior of people. For example, a Japanese woman once said to me, "Americans are so kind and helpful." I asked her what gave her that impression and she replied that an elderly woman on a bus had prevented her from falling. This Japanese woman took one incident that she experienced early on and applied it to the entire population. Remember that there is always a grain of truth in every stereotype.

American (Los Angeles) to Spain:

"I just LOVE how close things are in the city... you definitely don't need a car to get around most of the time. My nearest market is literally around the corner from my apartment, nearest bakery just a few steps from my door, and with a bank practically on every corner (well, at least one or two on practically every block), you can't complain about having difficult access to cash! I do LOVE this city!"

American to Thailand:

"I was shown about 8 different condos and apartments, all tall buildings in downtown area with fantastic views of the city, and all with excellent facilities like pool and exercise rooms. I will be able to find a place within walking distance of either the office, or a sky-train station that will get me to the office within minutes. The shopping is unbelievable. There are several malls and department stores within a two block radius of the office, not to mention the street vendors that are dotted around the area. There are plenty or restaurants and clubs in the area, even a Hard Rock Cafe."

The next phase is Degenerative. The **Degenerative** stage is when you start to realize that there are difficulties or challenges that come with this new assignment. At this stage, the prolonged stress (which is common during any learning curve) creates the physiological reaction of your body producing less white blood cells. As a result, your immune system is compromised. You, most probably, are more prone to catching a cold than anyone who is not in a situation similar to yours. And, sometimes it's tied in with a change of diet, one that is, albeit healthy, foreign to your system.

American to Peru:

"The health issues have also been a bit more obtrusive that I initially expected as I average about a day a month out sick from eating something I shouldn't have. No one else in my family has had quite the trouble I have, even after eating the exact same foods. I can't explain this but I will say that in the first 3 months in Peru I missed more work than I had in 7 years in Arizona."

American to Spain:

"Work has been VERY challenging. To some extent, I expected that already as it's a new job, but things have gotten complicated with some team members (I was not a welcomed arrival for my closest team members) and other developments, but also just trying to absorb all I need to learn has been like trying to drink from a fire hose! Way too much information to absorb at once!"

American to Switzerland:

"It is strange - I am finding that so many little things have been irritating me here!"

At roughly three to four months after your arrival, you enter into what is known as full-blown Culture Shock. Remember, **Culture Shock** is when your expectations do not meet the current reality. You are a fish out of water. It is not your desired environment.

American to Mexico:

"Another surprise is the corruption of the police...being stopped in your car for no violation and being asked to pay $2,700 pesos. We negotiated this down to $700 MXN but we should not have been extorted the money in the first place."

American to Puerto Rico (part of the USA):

"The island has been great, and no real issues with the culture. About the hardest part to deal with is driving. No big issues there either, just frustrating as people do whatever crazy thing comes to mind. Seeing 6 lanes of cars on a 2 lane highway is nothing unusual, nor is people backing-up a half mile on a freeway to get back to a missed exit. You have to let go of some of your expectations of order."

Culture Shock is comparable to a clinical depression for some, although in the list following these symptoms, you will notice how comparable they are to the listed reactions of the emotion anger. **Anger** is a secondary emotion to pain. *Pain is the primary emotion.* Anger is a self-defense mechanism to protect oneself from re-experiencing a pain.

While the vast majority of my clients go through this cycle of cultural adjustment, there is always the notable exception. Notice how this next executive's quote refers to the Cultural Adjustment Curve as "the curve of happiness." She is definitely an expat who sees the "glass half full," and her attitude has made her hugely successful in her assignment.

American to Switzerland:

"I always enjoy explaining the curve of happiness over time in the new country and they are very surprised to hear the information about the 4-month low point because it matches so well with how they are feeling. It was certainly true that knowing about it and expecting it made it much easier to deal with. And as for me, I am still in the tourist phase after 2 years![13] I cannot get enough of Europe and am still crazed with the lust to explore – I guess that's why I like it here so much."

---

[13] Still there 8 years later.

There are typically three types of symptoms that tend to occur during this period: 1) Physical, 2) Emotional, and 3) Behavioral.

1. **Physical.** These symptoms include the following:
   - Insomnia or excessive sleeping/chronic fatigue
   - Headaches (possibly tied into the knots in the back or sluggishness of blood circulation), backaches (muscle memory), stomach aches (excessive acid production from anxiety), etc.
   - Weight gain or loss (due to comfort food/drink or nervous energy)
   - Frequent illness/Absenteeism
   - Skin rashes

2. **Emotional.** These symptoms include the following:
   - Homesickness (longing for the familiar)
   - Depression
   - Irritability/Impatience
   - Anger (often misdirected or undirected)
   - Boredom
   - Withdrawal/Isolation/Detachment
   - Emotional outbursts/crying fits
   - Arrogance/Superiority Complex
   - Low self-esteem/Feelings of self-doubt
   - Feeling like a social reject

3. **Behavioral.** These symptoms include the following:
   - Bickering (with partners)
   - Silence (may indicate sadness/grieving)

- Loss of sense of humor
- Indecision/Confusion (which often turns into denial)
- Aggressive acts (e.g. road rage)
- Excessive cleaning
- Smoking/other drugs
- Excessive exercise
- Overindulging in food and drink or loss of appetite
- Excessive involvement in activities
- Blaming the locals
- Bargaining (making deals/promises or unrealistic attempts to make the situation go away)

How do you manage the adaptation process? Each person is unique. You must think of what strategies you have used previously to effectively deal with transitional change and seek out ways to adopt new methods of overcoming this stage. I always recommend that you attempt to establish and *develop a local support network* as quickly as possible.

Dane to USA:

"My wife Sonja is having a busy time supporting the whole family, - she has 3 daily trips to/from the school from 8 am to 2 pm and then supporting/entertaining the children at home afterwards. She gets very upset when friends from home say something like, 'Oh, but you are not working so you must have plenty of time to discover San Francisco!' She really hasn't had that so far but as the children get more and more integrated into the community I am convinced that this will also change over the next 2-6 months.

As expected, I am probably the one having the easiest time. I am working with people that I knew before coming here and I away from the home from 7 am to 6:30 pm and often have some work to do in the evenings, so my wife has most of the work with children alone."

With the advent of the webcam and internet capabilities, distance does not pose the same challenges today as it formerly did. Ideally, you will have a blend of locals, nationals, friends and colleagues from your last location; and, if you are overseas, a small coterie of expats. The one danger to be aware of in befriending expats is that if they have been in your locale for **less than two years**, as they *may* not have made it through the complete curve yet. If they have not, you run the risk of adding misery to your company.

What is the best way to break through this downturn in the curve? Much like how medical doctors treat you to alleviate your illness, you need to ameliorate your situation by getting some R&R (rest and relaxation). In psychology, this is called practicing *"escapism."* I advise that during this phase (3-4 months after your arrival), you arrange for a 10-day holiday/vacation to anywhere EXCEPT from your location of origin. While there are the rare survivors who defy this advice and make it through, your previous "home" is what I call "off limits." Think it through...if you feel depressed from being in your new environment, would you *really* want to come back to it from your comfortable environment? Could you truly be productively happy after leaving all those people who miss you and appreciate you? Going someplace new will offer you the R&R you need and deserve, and it appeals to your sense of wanderlust. Once you return back to your new "home," you have to do all of the things you normally do after a vacation, e.g. check the mail, fill up the fridge, wash the laundry, etc. And, what do you know? Home starts to feel like home.

Most people start an international assignment in September. This works well if you have children; but, if you count the months during this critical onboarding period, three months later you run into Christmas/Hanukkah. Most people wish to reunite with family during this holiday time. You do not want to mix the post-holiday blues with Culture Shock. If family and friends wish to visit you at ANY time during the first year of your assignment, the more the merrier. It's just that I recommend that you don't go back to your old "home." You require a full-immersion to make a healthy, transitional change.

American Family to Switzerland:

"We spent the last two weeks here in Europe. First, we visited the Christmas Market in Nuremberg, Germany--it was spectacular. The kids had a great time playing in snow and seeing all the Christmas booths and decorations around the city. We came back to Switzerland to open presents and then we flew to Rome for a few days. When we were looking for our ticket counter at the Rome airport, we passed an area that was for U.S. bound passengers. [My daughter] made the comment, 'I wish we could be one of these people,' and I realized that she was expressing how I felt as well. The good thing is that when we arrived back home in Vaud, it felt like home. The kids were happy to see their new toys, and [my husband] & I appreciated the comfort of our apartment. Just as you said, I think it was beneficial for us to go away to a strange locale to help us get assimilated to our new home."

American Family to England:

"Our first year in England went very well. The kids really adjusted better than we thought they would. Both Tom & Cynthia made lots of new friends and got involved in a number of extracurricular activities at school. As you indicated the day we met with you, I think it was very helpful that we arrived so late in the summer and within 2 weeks the kids began school. That way they got right into the swing of things."

One British couple accepted an expatriate assignment to California in September and they went back to England for the Christmas holiday season. It was at the end of that trip that the wife said that her husband (the employee) could return to California without her, and they would have an "intercontinental marriage." He came back to California without her, but he was miserable without her and did not complete his assignment. The aphorism holds true: "If Mama ain't happy, ain't nobody happy." *Spousal discontent is the number one reason why international assignments fail to be completed*. This is true even among Foreign Service Officers, whose spouses should expect to move a few times. Having said that, there are many couples who successfully manage to live and work separately for six months to two years.

After your return from your R&R vacation, your confidence and morale shoot up. There may be a set-back along the way – which is indicated on the curve, but it continues to progress upwards to the final stage: **Full Acceptance**. Typically, one can arrive at this stage at anywhere from 9-12 months if s/he has been attempting a complete immersion. It is at this stage that you can pretty objectively make comparisons about what the benefits and disadvantages are of each your original and new locations. It is at this point that I suggest a return to your old home to visit family and friends. Some people might need 1.5-2 years to reach this stage. The longer time frame may have been due to an earlier than recommended trip to the old home. After two years, Full Acceptance becomes less likely with time, and I've seen it take up to six years for completion of this curve.

American to Spain:

"We have the kiss-kiss greeting down pat and we never dine and dash! I would say that we have integrated into school and work, and to a lesser extent, socially. I have made some friends here and developed relationships with 'cultural informants.' We are much more flexible about time now. I am content right now, but the first few months were very draining for me. There was a lot to do, and the whole family counted on my language skills for every encounter."

Americans to England:

"London is a great city to live in, albeit an expensive one. The biggest surprise to me is how crude the concept of customer service is here. In over 90% of buying situations, the provider seems totally uninterested in making a sale, nor do they do anything to help you with your purchases. That extends to government institutions, where the bureaucracy is monumentally crushing. I have never been in these types of situations where it takes tons of paperwork and weeks to complete simple transactions that in the states are practically instantaneous (parking permits, banking accounts, etc.). So patience, not one of my strong points, has been tested and extended on more than one occasion. There have been a few other surprises, like TV licenses, but also a number of pleasantries, like decent food in restaurants, and great places to visit and things to see. Also, seeing the world through the eyes of non-Americans is always different and interesting."

American to Switzerland:

"I found that if you don't want to change your lifestyle, you can keep doing the same things as in the US because everything is available here, it's just much more expensive to keep the same lifestyle. We have opted for the "When in Rome..." idea. So I have kept our very small freezer within our small refrigerator and go grocery shopping about 2-3 times a week like locals do. I even walk to the grocery store - which of course is unheard of back home. We don't have a microwave, our food is fresh (which they are big on here) and I cook almost every night. Initially I refused to buy anything we didn't need because it's SO expensive but I've gotten used to the prices and have even purchased clothing."

Others may have never come out of Culture Shock. This is indicated by the horizontal line. I call these people the flatliners. **Flatliners** are so angry at their situation that they feel comfort with others who they perceive as being in a similar situation and tend to congregate with them. This way, they do not feel as though they are "wrong" or the "social outcast" and they find comfort in numbers. This is where people flock to live in communities that resemble their old home. For example, there exists a suburb outside of Tokyo where Americans have homes built into a similar format of Knott's Landing.[14] And, of course, in the United States we have our Chinatowns, etc., where the inhabitants don't really have to learn English because they can get everything they need by staying in that little bubble. It is safe there.

Physical signs of anger are common for those who are stuck in this stage. These can include:

- Heightened blood pressure

- Increase of stress hormones

- Shortness of breath

- Heart palpitations

---

[14] Knott's Landing was a popular TV series in the '80s of life in the suburbs on a street with a cul-de-sac.

- Trembling
- Heightened senses
- Dulled senses
- Stiffness of posture
- Dilated pupils
- Increased physical strength
- Speech and motion are faster and more intense
- Tense muscles
- Impotence

Here are some behaviors and feelings related to anger:

- Criticism
- Irritation
- Hatred
- Silence
- Passive Aggressive Behavior
- Ill-will
- Resentment/Bitterness
- Envy
- Jealousy
- Insecurity
- Low self-esteem
- Self-loathing
- Judgmental
- Condemning
- Malaise
- Depression

- Anxiety

- Apathy

- Sleeplessness

Self-awareness is crucial to surviving this cultural adjustment curve. It would be prudent to be aware of where you are on the curve so you can strategize the best way through it. *Assess your personal priorities* and *develop a strategic plan* that allows you to focus on where you want to go and what you want to accomplish. Those who fail to plan, plan to fail. Write it down. New Age theory dictates that if it's on paper, the universe will cooperate. What do you have to lose?

Visualization boards are a great project for either yourself and/or your family. These are charts, pin-up boards, or sheets of paper that reflect (usually with pictures) what you want most out of life. There doesn't have to be a time limit on it — it's just something that you would like to do, have, or experience.

Understanding the cultural adjustment curve will help you move through many stresses in life. I enjoy using the analogy of the birth of a child. Prior to the infant's arrival, you may experience excitement of the pregnancy and anxiety over the baby's health or the delivery, for example. Upon Junior's arrival, you may experience the "Tourist/Honeymoon" stage of how wonderful it is to be a parent. Then, the degeneration sets in. This is the difficulty of learning how to care for an infant. Culture Shock hits after so many sleepless nights and possibly not finding an adequate or trustworthy babysitter (or not being able to let go!). At some point, you emerge from that depth in the curve and possibly suffer a setback (e.g. child becomes ill), and then you progress to the last stage of "Full Acceptance." It is at this final stage that you may contemplate having another child or feel quite confident in your parenting skills. The point of this analogy is that every time life throws you a curve, whether it be a new job, marriage, relocation, or the death of a loved one, you do need time to fully acknowledge the emotion and then, by implementing your survival skills, move past those emotions.

Knowledge (preparation or experience), skills (emotional, coping, strategy), attitude (resilience, that can-do-it ability, bounceback imperviousness) and self-awareness are critical in your success of the curve. Remember to reward yourself for moving in the direction that is productive for you.

American to Switzerland:

"There are a few things I distinctly remember we should have done.

For us, the first month was the toughest. Not having our 'stuff' was very depressing. It was 6 weeks after we arrived before we received our shipment. There are 2 shipments, the flight and the boat. [The company] allots a flight shipment (which takes 4 weeks to arrive) for expats from the US. Ignore their recommendation. The first thing I highly recommend for families, especially with kids, is to have their BOAT shipment picked up from the US 8 weeks before they are due to arrive here. Yes, it can be done, they just have to push. That way, when they get here, instead of being depressed and frustrated about being in a different country where they can't communicate well and don't know where to go to get whatever they need, they can be focused on putting their house together, getting settled as fast as possible so that a 'normal' routine can be established right away. We stayed in our apartment with temporary furniture and had to buy 'temporary' items to get through. No matter what you pack on the flight shipment, it's not enough, and one will tend to forget a very important item, ours was 'tools.' I think it's better to be at a hotel in a place where you know where to get things you need and where you're not feeling out of sorts yet.

Second, we sold most of the kids stuff and decided that we would just buy here, and although we're okay now, it was so stressful in the beginning because everything here is so expensive, and we couldn't get quite exactly what we wanted. Most pieces of furniture are very low and we personally do not like them. Also, everything closes early and Sundays are out. So the time you have to go shopping is very limited. I suggest buy all that you want as far as furniture is concerned and have it shipped. And if they're going to Geneva, buy bathroom and kitchen storage units and light fixtures, as you might already know, they take these with them when they move out. This goes with the whole getting settled deal.

Third, there are small items that we all like. Personal stuff. Mine happens to be really good hand / body lotion, the wipes at Costco, arts and crafts for the kids, the baking ingredients, and more importantly, for the kids, the medicines that they are familiar with. For fever, they use suppositories, the kids are, of course, not used to that, and I only had 1 bottle of Motrin. I suggest, unless they know where to get these things where they are going, to stock-up before they leave. I know it sounds weird, but for example, most lotion here is very silky/oily and does not absorb properly on the skin, the wipes don't have white cover on top, so they tend to dry out and are not really portable like the Costco ones. Baking products have different percentage of the ingredients. They cook differently. [My husband] has had to bake things at least twice to get them to come out right. We had to have some items shipped. Other things you can't get here; vanilla extract, good pancake mix, the brownie mix, cranberry juice (for a Cosmopolitan). At least for the first 2 months, anyone moving here should bring / stock-up on all their comfort foods / items. I had things shipped, and it wasn't worth it.

And finally, take as many language lessons at home as possible. Fully immerse if you can. The teachers here are great but if you can speak and understand when you arrive, then you won't feel as out of place. There won't be this, 'I'm afraid to say anything because I don't want to make a fool of myself' deal. Oh, and if they are (from the same company), see if they can log on to the (company) expat site so they can get suggestions from other expats."

CHAPTER 6

CULTURAL FUNDAMENTALS

Words are symbols. We have to figure out which words strung together make us the most effective. If a certain combination of words or letters evokes the "wrong" reaction, then we search to course correct. This is why so many of us find pleasure in seeking out the expletives, or "bad" words, when we learn a new language – we are tickled that a string of letters that bears no meaning to us has *power* over someone else – the power, that is, to cause a reaction. It is, usually, not so funny when it is in our own language.

An Ecuadorean told me the story of how he overheard some Americans[15]* speaking in the hallway at work. One of them was talking about how he was tired of these "f*%#ing Ecuadoreans." This executive asked me what I believed would prompt an American to make such a remark. Instead of repeating the expletive verbatim in my response, I exchanged it with "f-ing Ecuadoreans." As I said it, he interjected, "Why didn't you just say the word? Why did you change it?" While the word did not have the same impact for him, I also had to model how the word would be used in mixed American company that might find the phrase offensive, even when it is repeated by another source. The impact of the word can be strong, and offensive, to native ears.

---

[15] The usage of the term "Americans" is meant to represent those from the United States. The author recognizes that other nationalities from North America, Central and South America can also be recognized as Americans.

Many words have origins that stem from marginalization. For example, for centuries the word "left" used to carry a much more negative connotation than present day; whereas, "right" carries a positive connotation of "correctness" and "righteousness." Until the 1960's in the USA, Catholic nuns used a wooden ruler to swat the hands of children in school who wrote with their left-hands. In French ("gauche") and Italian ("sinistra"), the word "left" has come to mean "tacky" and "sinister" respectively. Today, radical thought is considered "left-wing." Another example is the word "pagan" that is commonly used as a synonym for devil worship. The origin is from the Latin word "paganus" which means "country-dweller." Pagans were the rural folk who practiced Nature worship, much like Native Americans. That practice was considered evil, since the country-dwellers were not indoctrinated into Christianity.

The word **stereotype** comes from Greek origin, meaning "solid kind." Stereotype was coined in the printing world, as it was the typographical element used for newspapers and non-electric typewriters. In today's world, when we think of the word stereotype, we think of it as one statement that is applied to every member of a particular culture. For example, "That's just the way women are," or "All Asians are good in Math," or "Jews don't eat pork." I always get, "You must be a fantastic dancer, being that you're half-Cuban and half-Colombian!" Yes, I can keep a beat without use of a metronome, but since I was raised strict Protestant, I am by no means Shakira.

This is what you can remember about stereotypes:

- Rigid and fixed - assumes every member of a culture is virtually identical

- Emotive and judgmental

- Impede learning

Generalizations make use of qualifiers to avoid the oversimplification of stereotypes. **Qualifiers** are words that define the quality of the statement. Examples of qualifiers include: most, many, tend to, a lot, some, a few, in general, several, the majority, etc. For example, "Most Scandinavians are blonde." This does not mean that all are blonde. There are several brunettes, a lot of redheads, and a few raven-haired ones. The usage of generalizations allows for the following:

- Individual differences - avoids oversimplification

- Broad guidelines

- Tentative and relative language

- Facilitate learning

Ethnocentrism is the belief that one particular culture is the "right" one. Literally, it is the "centering," or focus, on one "ethnicity." Human beings have a tendency to be tribal. They affiliate themselves depending on the opposing group. We unite as Americans when confronted with another national group. If we are among ourselves, we might differentiate ourselves by region (e.g. East Coast rappers vs West Coast rappers) and/or state (e.g. California vs Washington). If we focus on intrastate, then there is the differentiation of city (e.g. Los Angeles vs San Francisco – it seems if you love one, you hate the other). Once in the city, the focus is on neighborhood (e.g. Manhattan Beach vs Venice Beach). And so on, and so forth. We have incidents where there is a culture clash within Jewish schools because a sizable minority is Persian Jewish and the rest are Jews from a variety of national backgrounds. Bear these thoughts in mind the next time you attempt, in earnest faith, to push two colleagues from Peru and Chile together *just because* they speak Spanish and/or happen to be from South America. There is national history that may separate those two from wishing to speak with each other.

For ethnocentrism, the usage creates the following:

- Maintains perspective that one's own culture is the "right" one

- Judgmental and divisive

- Can use a combination of stereotypes and generalizations in speech

CHAPTER 7

COMMUNICATION

Europeans find the following quote as funny:
"I speak Spanish to God,
Italian to women,
French to men,
and German to my horse."
    – Charles V, King of Spain (1516-1522)

What many Europeans do not find interesting is what they perceive as the American obsession with being politically correct. They believe you have an opinion and they feel that you are "keeping that window hidden" (see Johari Window) by not sharing with them what you believe. They realize that you are the product of your culture, so they are testing to see if you float with the current thought that pertains to your culture. What they really want to see is your logic, the way you think. If your logic is sound, then they can respect it *even if* they wholeheartedly disagree with it, and may attack it vehemently. Quips, like the one above made by King Charles, are meant to have each nationality laugh at its reputation. They appear as stereotypes and are accepted as generalizations. The following joke is similar by comparison:

What is the difference between Heaven and Hell?

In Heaven,
The cooks are Italian,

The policemen are English,

The lovers are French,

The mechanics are German,

And the whole thing is organized by the Swiss.

In Hell,

The cooks are English,

The policemen are German,

The lovers are Swiss,

The mechanics are French,

And the whole thing is organized by the Italians.[16]

Humor is one of the last variables understood in culture because it is tied into psychology; and, since we are raised in different socio-cultural environs, it is often difficult to understand why/how another cultural group finds something so funny when you do not consider the scenario funny whatsoever. What is interesting to note is that much of American humor is targeted at the misfortune of *others*. We laugh at someone tripping or experiencing a rather serious accident. This type of mentality may lock us into a mindset against being capable of laughing at ourselves.

Taboo subjects of conversation are those topics which are not spoken about openly. I call them "hot topics." Whether as a serious topic of discussion or in jest, please refrain from topics regarding **sex, politics, or religion** here in the USA. Examples include, Pro-Life/Pro-Choice, the Right to Bear Arms, School Prayer, etc. These are taboo subjects in the USA that, once addressed, may lead to irreparable perceptions and credibility. For example, many cultures around the world view the USA as hypocritical because the image projected is Puritanical but the actions are nothing close, so they may ask

---

[16] Anonymous.

questions or make comments which are typically perceived as offensive.

<u>Belgian to USA</u>:

"Yes, we heard about the taboo subjects from our Belgian colleague in New Jersey. He said he invited his American work colleague and his wife over for dinner. Since we, as Belgians, find politics a lively topic for discussion, he talked about how much he disliked US foreign policy. The next day, the Americans called to say, 'Thank you for dinner. We will never go to your house again.'"

An Argentine once described to me how he was in a group of colleagues at one of his co-worker's home on the weekend. They had gathered to watch soccer. When the game began, he exclaimed, "I don't want to watch women play!" He was stunned to have the group "turn" on him. Only one (a man) spoke up to say, "I feel that way, too, but I didn't want to say it." The question posed by the Argentine was, "Why don't people say what they honestly think and/or feel?" Cultures not practiced in being politically correct find this behavior to be dishonest and do not wish to be associated with what they describe as groupthink. **Groupthink** is when the members of a group exhibit a type of thought that develops into behavior/speech and is delivered in a way to try to minimize conflict and reach consensus. It's usually committed without analyzing or evaluating ideas.

The Cuban Missile Crisis, during the Kennedy Administration, was a crisis purportedly averted by an acknowledgment of groupthink and the efforts made by President John F. Kennedy (JFK) to avoid the process from repeating itself. President Kennedy noticed that his assembled advisors were deferential and possibly agreeing with the hierarchy so as to be supportive insiders and trusted group members; not opponents. Therefore, JFK removed himself from the meetings and left his brother in charge. The changes made in the group dynamics allowed for more honest revelation of thought and advisements. They felt safe to speak up, and not openly contradict their leader.

Irving Janis, expert on groupthink, lists seven ways to avoid groupthink behavior:[17]

1. **Critical Evaluator**. Leaders should assign each member the role of "critical evaluator." This allows each member to freely air objections and doubts.

2. **Hierarchical Role**. Higher-ups should not express an opinion when assigning a task to a group.

3. **Diverse Task Teams**. The organization should set up several independent groups, working on the same problem.

4. **Open Consideration**. All effective alternatives should be examined.

5. **Internal Consultant**. Each member should discuss the group's ideas with trusted people outside of the group.

6. **External Consultant**. The group should invite outside experts into meetings. Group members should be allowed to discuss with and question the outside experts.

7. **Devil's Advocate**. At least one group member should be assigned the role of Devil's Advocate. It should be a different person for each meeting.

Since we have already established that we all bring our prior associations to the communication process, we must acknowledge that pure communication is impossible. I laugh when I remember the time my mother tried to express to my husband, "In Colombia, they call me María Antonia. Here, they call me María alone." With her

---

[17] Janis, Irving. *Victims of Groupthink*. Boston: Houghton Mifflin Company. pp. 209-215.

accent and her incorrect syntax, my husband repeated what he thought he heard, "They call you María Alón??" "Yes," said my mother, nodding a confirmation. It took me, as a third-party observer, to inform both of them that they were not having a conversation. "They *only* call her Maria," I informed my husband. Many Spanish-speaking and Chinese cultures have two first names, but Americans are accustomed to using only one, leaving members of these nationalities feeling a bit robbed of their complete identity.

COMMUNICATION – INDIRECT

We communicate in many ways; much of it unconscious. In fact, 55% is body language, 38% is vocal, and a mere 7% is words.

BODY LANGUAGE

Aside from the aforementioned universal emotions that register on a person's face, there are several forms of communication conveyed by body language or related behaviors. Note the following examples with the applied terminology for reference:

Chromatics	Communication through use of **colors**. E.g. red roses mean love, while yellow roses mean friendship.
Chronemics	Communication through use of **time** within a culture. E.g. being 10 minutes late to a business meeting is disrespectful in the USA, but being 10 minutes late to a dinner in someone's home is respectful.
Haptics	Communication through the use of **bodily contact**. E.g. touching the arm conveys warmth and sincerity in the USA, or it is a sexual overture.
Kinesics	Communication through **body movements**, including facial expression, gestures, and posture. E.g. a smile

	could signal enjoyment, a greeting, embarrassment, etc.
Oculesics	Communication through **eye contact** and gaze. E.g. a held gaze could be interpreted as a sexual overture in the USA, a stare down, or veracity.
Proxemics	Communication through the use of **space**. E.g. too far away can be interpreted as disinterest, while too close can be interpreted as threatening or sexually interest. Naturally, this is relative.

Japanese to USA:

"I happened to meet several new people in the past week, so I had a chance to try the 'strong' handshake, and now I know what you mean!"

If you are aware of the expectations of the culture you are entering, then you are enabled to work within the "reward band." Remember, culture shock occurs when expectations are not met.

Several misunderstandings develop because of proxemics. The values are Private Space and Public Space. For example, Brazilians – who are known for the body contact dance *lambada*, among other things – have a tendency to sit and stand quite close (relatively speaking from an American standpoint) to others. Depending on the person, or gender, you may feel inclined to stay put or back off. The backing off would convey a message, most likely, to the Brazilian that would lead to some confusion. For an American third-party observer, s/he might believe that the closeness indicates sexual interest. This is what is called that person's "cultural baggage" or "frame of reference"—which is how one sees the world from his/her experience or conditioning. S/He is looking at the situation without considering other possible interpretations. It is, again, "the young lady & the old lady" (pg 1).

VOCAL

How we say *what we say* matters. Volume, intonation, inflection, speed, timing, use of silence, and sounds that are not words (such as *hmmm* and *ah*) fall into this category. Mandarin, for example, has four tonal variants that can distinguish a monosyllabic word to have a distinct meaning. In fact, one word can be constructed to form a sentence, using 3 out of the 4 tones: Mā mà mǎ (Mother curses the horse). In American English,[18] we use tones; however, they are generally used over the course of the sentence, and the emphasis on certain words changes the meaning from a statement to a question: "He is coming." versus "He is coming?" If the recipient/listener is an expert in English but not in tones, the meaning is lost. Consider the following exact same sentence as an example:

1. ***Where*** did you get that? (Location is important)
2. Where did ***you*** get that? (Shock/surprise the person could acquire the widget)
3. Where did you get ***that***? (Shock/surprise at the widget acquired)

So if someone in another continent cannot see your face for additional visual cues and hears, "Can you help me?" S/He may be confused because the question could be heard as any one of the following:

1. ***Can*** you help me?" (Unsure of the assistance being possible)

---

[18] I say "American English" because the British strongly feel that Americans speak a different language than "English." This comes from many differences in language, not just from contractions (e.g. "can't," instead of "cannot," etc.)

2. Can **you** help me?" (Unsure of the person being the one to ask)

3. Can you **help** me?" (Desperation, anger)

4. Can you help **me**?" (Directive – wants immediate help to the individual)

CHAPTER 8

FACE SAVING

Most cultures around the world employ a face saving technique. The fact is, we Americans, do, too – just not to the degree some others do. In work, we expect "yes" to mean "yes." Socially, however, we might fib or tell a "white lie" to avoid embarrassment either on our part, or to spare the other person embarrassment. Having said that, expect cultures from most of Asia, Latin America, the Middle East, Africa, and the Mediterranean to practice saving face.

In these face saving cultures, "yes" shows respect – it may not be an actual fact. It can mean "I hear you," "I understand," "I follow what you're saying." A real "yes" is usually backed up with details.

Americans fall in between the spectrum of direct and indirect communicators. So, Americans get frustrated by the Japanese "hai"- which means "yes," thinking that they have established an agreement; and embarrassed, perhaps, by the German who showed up on their doorstep because the American casually said, "Whenever you're in the neighborhood, stop by and say hi." When Dietlind did just that, her co-worker opened his door and said, "What are you doing here?"

Saying "no" in face saving cultures comes out indirectly. So as not to offend you, the answer may be "It is difficult," or "It is not convenient." It is at this point that you must understand to shy away from your request. That would demonstrate a gracious understanding and it takes the recipient off the hook from having to displease you.

The response, "Yes, but there may be problems," usually means no. Any "yes, but" comments typically mean no. Sucking in of air through teeth, as done in Asia, is a non-verbal "no." Sometimes questions/requests are ignored by pretending that the question/request was not heard or that they don't understand. Face-savers may talk around the question/request in a circumloquacious manner just to try and throw you off the topic and hope that you get the hint.

<u>American to Mexico:</u>

"For me, being down here has been great. All the little issues that come up don't mean a thing when I think about the experience that we are all having and the positives that will come out of this when the assignment is over. I remember you telling us that Mexicans have a difficult time saying 'no' or that they don't want to disappoint. I have certainly come across this from a work perspective. It has actually cost us (the company) time and money. When I relayed your explanation to the locals that I'm working with, it made sense and they agreed."

Many Americans ask "Why?" Why do these saving face cultures do what they do? I have come up with four basic reasons why certain cultures practice face saving techniques. They...

1. **Don't have an answer, but they want to give you one.** (Cooperation)

   People often ask, "Why is it that when I travel to Mexico, the people are so friendly, but when I ask them for directions, they give me the wrong ones?"

2. **Have an answer, but it's not what you want to hear.** (Harmony)

An American expatriate[19] (expat) in Venezuela took his company car to the company mechanic on a Tuesday. He asked the mechanic if the car would be ready on Friday. The mechanic answered "yes." When the American dropped by on Friday to pick up the car, the mechanic said it would not be ready until Monday. The American asked, "Well, why did you tell me it would be ready on Friday, then?" The response was, "It is a question of happiness...instead of six days of being upset, you were happy for three days."

3. **Have an answer, but politics** (Hierarchy) **won't allow them to tell you.**

I once facilitated an inter-regional department meeting where this popped up. The USA office had its product being developed in Mexico. The American asked the Mexican, "Why didn't you respond to my email?" The Mexican (context is important here) picked up his pen, kept his eyes focused on it while he rotated and responded with his head down, "Because I didn't get it." Right there, it was apparent to anyone from a High Context culture (as it was for the one Indian in the room), that the Mexican did, in fact, get the email, but he felt that something or someone was preventing him from disclosing information at that time and/or in that particular setting. I discovered after the meeting that the Mexican's boss had had an argument with the American's boss.

4. **Have an answer, but don't want to embarrass anyone.** (Social Politics/Collectivism)

---

[19] An **expatriate** is someone who leaves his/her country to work in another country. Americans leaving to work abroad are expatriates. An **inpatriate** is someone from another country who enters your country (legally) to work. A **repatriate** is someone who was working abroad and has returned to his/her country of origin.

Since the Koreans are a highly collective society, relying on the group and sparing the group from embarrassment is paramount. So, when the American manager went over to check on production and discovered an error, he wanted to know who was to blame. The team leader eventually stepped forward and said that his team was responsible. The American wanted an individual's name. He was again told that the team is to be held accountable, but because of the American's persistence, he was told that that person had quietly resigned by going home.

Notice the four values of Cooperation, Harmony, Hierarchy, and Collectivism. These values are preferred more by women than by men. As a result, women, more so than men, may practice face-saving for these same reasons in the USA.

American to Mexico:

"Culturally, you can not underestimate the amount of times people will give you the answer you want to hear vs the correct answer. 'I'll get it done in time.' Simple examples include if you want your dry cleaning for a business trip by Wednesday...the dry cleaning is never done when they say or if you want directions for a location, many times you get a wrong answer vs a person just saying 'I don't know.' At work this is frustrating as well. As a result, one needs to follow up 4-5 times to make sure things are done on time. It can be exhausting and being nice only means some people take advantage of you longer."

An example that incorporates all of the abovementioned values of Cooperation, Harmony, Hierarchy, and Collectivism is when Dutch missionaries went to Indonesia. The missionaries told the parable of Jesus (Matthew 21:28-32). In this parable, Jesus spoke of a man who had two sons. The father asked one son to work in the field and the son said he *wouldn't* go, but ended up going (Task-orientation). The father asked the other son and the son said he *would* go (Relationship-orientation), but didn't end up going. Jesus' question was, "Which son did his father's will?" Now, mind you, Jesus never gave answers to his parables. The Dutch would argue that it is the son who worked in the field who did his father's will. The Indonesians would argue that it is the son who said "yes" to his father who did his father's will. Now imagine this scenario occurring in your workplace!

The Japanese are known for avoiding conflict. This has been the source of much Japanese drama for ages. The Japanese have conflict with *honne* (true feelings kept hidden) and *giri* (social obligations). *Tatemae* (which means "façade") is the behavior and opinions that one publicly presents and does not necessarily match the *honne*. To an American, the Japanese appear as "yes-men" and/or dishonest.

I lunched with two of my Japanese clients at the Cheesecake Factory here in California. The Cheesecake Factory is renown for serving "healthy" (read: American or huge) portions. At the end of my meal, I requested a "doggy bag."[20] I asked my Japanese lunchmates if they had heard of the doggy bag. Yes, they replied, and asked to offer an explanation. They said, "It is not that you are going to eat the remainder of the food tonight. It is that you wish to spare the chef humiliation from not eating his food." What Japanese cultural baggage! I had to inform them, "No offense to the chef. But, I don't know him/her and I most probably will eat this tonight to save myself time from cooking after my long commute home. I paid for this food and I want it!" They were stunned to think anyone would eat leftovers, but bear in mind they come from a culture where the price

---

[20] The doggy bag is another American cultural idiosyncracy. It is rumored to be catching on in other cultures, though. It is a practice still considered in most countries to be embarrassing.

of fish drops with each hour of the day, as the fresh catch has the most quality. Rice is always made fresh. Refrigerators are much smaller around the world.

There are three main ways to practice indirect communication:

1. **Mediation** – This is practiced when a third person is used as a go-between. Emotions such as embarrassment, intimidation, anger, etc. are usually involved that would prompt mediation. It is a face-saving measure.

2. **Refraction** – This is practiced when statements intended for one person are made to another, while that first person is present. For example, this behavior can be heard in classrooms as a form of positive reinforcement. Some teachers recognize a child for his/her behavior, but mentions it to the class: "I like the way Susie is sitting quietly with her desk clean."

   One of my clients from Australia experienced Refraction during her first week on the job in California. A French woman (apparently stuck in the Culture Shock phase) approached her to complain loudly about Americans. The Australian was embarrassed by the behavior because she felt that the Americans in the surrounding cubicles could hear the complaints. She felt this was the intent of the French woman and couldn't understand the cause.

3. **Covert Revelation** – This is practiced when the instigator portrays him/herself as the messenger of another; and/or allows some kind of self-communication. In the former case, this method is usually practiced by those fearful of rejection...they are, in essence, testing the waters by pretending it was the actions of someone else. In the latter case, notes/diaries are discovered or corners of magazines are dog-eared with items circled.

CHAPTER 9

COMMUNICATION- DIRECT

To reiterate, words are symbols. They represent meaning. We deliver meaning to attain our Needs and Wants. Therefore, they must be selected carefully. I wondered who the Cultural Advisors to President George W. Bush were when he first referred to Operation Iraqi Freedom as "Operation Crusade." "Crusade" is not the optimal choice to use for a culture where the Crusades are a part of the past that reaches the present for the Middle East. Using words of war contributes toward creating more of what is communicated (e.g. religious assault); it does not contribute towards eliminating war. Also, word selection shows thought process...Is it the Persian Gulf or Arabian Gulf? Is it the Falkland Isles or Las Malvinas?

> German to USA:
>
> "In my marketing meeting, someone in my group wrote up on the dry-erase board on one side 'USA' and on the other side 'ROW.'[21] I know Germany is not a large enough country to compete as a region against the US, but at least lump us in as part of a continent and not ROW !"

> Many Cultures to USA:
>
> "Why do Americans ask, 'How are you?' and then don't wait for the answer?"

---

[21] ROW = Rest of World

Idioms are ubiquitous in American English, and they are very difficult for non-native speakers to understand. I have served as a mediator for face-saving cultures. Here are some of the comments they are happy to finally say indirectly through mediation:

"HQ is not understanding the burden everyone has of doing everything in English. It is intimidating, exasperating, and we (the Japanese) don't like to make mistakes."

"If you don't speak up, you might as well not even be there."

"What is missing is that (people at HQ) need to write a memo summarizing the main points. We get a lot of verbal (instructions) and PowerPoints."

<u>American to Switzerland:</u>

"I didn't realize how much we use generalities or 'manners of saying' in the American culture. Language is by far has been the biggest challenge. It is difficult to conduct the daily/weekly chores of life and not speak German. Most individuals in the grocery stores or department stores will tell you they don't speak English. In many cases they speak it well enough to communicate, but in their culture, if you have not 'mastered' the language then you don't speak the language. In several other cases though, they really don't speak English so my very broken French has gotten me through some situations. Language is not a problem at all for work but even there with such an international group there are differences in the use of words."

Most of the following idioms are commonly used in U.S. business and are <u>not</u> readily understood by foreign counterparts:

Games/Sports
Across the board
Ahead of the game

At this stage of the game

Break even

Have two strikes against you

Carry/Drop the ball

Get the ball rolling

Keep the ball rolling

Games at which two can play

Lay one's cards on the table

Your turn up to bat

Jump the gun

Military-related expressions

All systems go

Dead in the water

Dropped a bomb

Head off

Hold the line

In the line of duty

Join forces

Line of fire

Lose ground

Quick on the trigger

Under fire

Time

Against the clock

Ahead of time

Better late than never

Call it a day

Early bird catches the worm

Less than no time

Make a day of it

Put it on the back burner

Other

Beat around the bush

Eighty-six it

Freehand/free rein

Get the point

Get right on it

Get this wrapped up

Go out of one's way

Have a hand in

Have it coming

Hold one's own

Knock on wood

In the face of

Press one's luck

Put all one's eggs in one basket

Put one's best foot forward

Roll up one's sleeves

Remember, English can be hard even for some native speakers. Try reading the following statements aloud:

- The soldier decided to desert his dessert in the desert.

- Since there is no time like the present, he said it was time to present the present.

- When shot at, the dove dove into the bushes.

- The farm was used to produce produce.

When speaking with someone who is **ESL** (English as a Second Language), keep these following points in mind:

- Avoid slang, jargon, idioms, and colloquialisms.

- Restate key points.

- Use short and easily defined phrases.

- Give the speaker enough time to finish speaking.

- Do not cover too much information at once.

- Do not restate the same message loudly. Beware of your tone of voice. Do not speak to them like children.

- Do not take it personally.

- Do not take a "yes" for an answer. Probe for understanding!

- Paraphrase for understanding.

- Be patient.

- Follow up with an e-mail.

- Share the responsibility for good or poor communication.

<u>American to Switzerland</u>:

"Every day at work I hear people speaking French, German, Italian, Spanish, Portuguese, Russian, Polish, Hindi, and English. It truly is an international workplace. I have two important learnings from my experience, so far, that I will take with me from this experience:

Learning #1: English is not the mother-tongue for many of the people that I am in contact with everyday. I have learned the importance of slowing down my speech and even trying to use easier vocabulary when communicating. I tend to speak faster when really interested/excited about a topic, but this isn't fair for the audience, because they have a harder time understanding. Since I am still new to French, I can identify with people who have English as a secondary language. I feel like my English is not as strong as before my assignment, but I think that it only feels that way because it is hard to describe things sometimes without using slang.

Learning #2: Since English is not the first language of most people that I am in contact with, they may come across in a way that may seem offensive or rude. This may be because they don't express themselves well in English or they are translating directly word-for-word from their mother-tongue. Here is a simplified example, someone who speaks Russian as their first language may say "What !!!"[22] if they don't understand you. Even though you are told in the US when you are growing up that this is considered rude, this is the exact translation from what is said in Russian. It may sound harsh or rude when you hear it, but it isn't intended to be. I try to utilize patience, which is easier in person or on the phone, but with e-mail communication, I sometimes forget this fact and need to take a deep breath before responding.

These two learnings will probably prove valuable when dealing with people in the future as I progress down the management track."

Be aware of schedule differences. Some companies forget what the time zone differences are. A great website is www.timeanddate.com. Go to World Clock Meeting Planner. Green shades normal business hours. Yellow shades after hours. Mauve shades sleeping hours. Face-saving cultures will not complain and attend a teleconference during sleeping hours. And remember, they have to deal with English as a Second Language, on top of feeling exhausted and sleepy – not to mention, lack of consideration to the time zone differences. As a demonstration of this online tool, I entered Los Angeles, Paris, and Bangkok.

---

[22] Some Americans when living abroad interestingly begin to pick up British punctuation style, which is taught throughout the world. In British English, a space is left between the last word and the exclamation mark or question mark.

Los Angeles	Paris	Bangkok
Mon 9:00 AM	Mon 6:00 PM	Midnight Mon-Tue
Mon 10:00 AM	Mon 7:00 PM	Tue 1:00 AM
Mon 11:00 AM	Mon 8:00 PM	Tue 2:00 AM
Mon 12:00 Noon	Mon 9:00 PM	Tue 3:00 AM
Mon 1:00 PM	Mon 10:00 PM	Tue 4:00 AM
Mon 2:00 PM	Mon 11:00 PM	Tue 5:00 AM
Mon 3:00 PM	Midnight Mon-Tue	Tue 6:00 AM
Mon 4:00 PM	Tue 1:00 AM	Tue 7:00 AM
Mon 5:00 PM	Tue 2:00 AM	Tue 8:00 AM
Mon 6:00 PM	Tue 3:00 AM	Tue 9:00 AM
Mon 7:00 PM	Tue 4:00 AM	Tue 10:00 AM
Mon 8:00 PM	Tue 5:00 AM	Tue 11:00 AM
Mon 9:00 PM	Tue 6:00 AM	Tue 12:00 Noon

CHAPTER 10

HIGH/LOW CONTEXT COMMUNICATION

High Context communicators read between lines. These communicators may have more potential to excel at the whole pie of communication, i.e. words, vocal, and body language. They are adept at determining the congruency of the message. However, there is always room for misinterpretation.

<u>Italian to USA</u>:

"The waitress brought me the bill. I paid it. When I started to leave, she came after me and said, 'You were supposed to leave 15% !' I told her, 'I'm sorry. I was hungry !'"[23]

<u>High Context Cultures</u> (information is Implicit and Indirect) ↓

Japanese
Chinese
Indian
Russian
Arab
Greek
Latin American
Spanish

---

[23] The USA is the *only* country that does not have the tip built into the tip. This leaves many cultures with the perception that Americans are *so* wealthy that we unload our cash on the table and leave it.

Italian

French   ↕

Belgian-French

French-Canadian

English

English Canadian

Australian

American

Scandinavian

Belgian-Flemish

German

Swiss German

<u>Low Context Cultures</u> (information is Explicit and Direct) ↑

The Japanese are at the High end (High Context). They have several words in Japanese that reflect the culture around this concept. For example, *"ishin denshin"* basically means "intuitive understanding." There are no words or signs. From an American point of view (POV), it is like telepathic communication. It is communicating viscerally as "belly-talk" – the literally translated word for *haragei*. One example is when my Japanese co-worker, Akahana, went back to Japan with her American husband to visit her family. Suddenly, she found herself being scolded by her mother in the kitchen. Her mother expected Akahana to practice *ishin denshin*. What exactly were these expectations? Her mother felt that Akahana's brother, father, and husband were "busy" relaxing after supper; so Akahana should have known through *haragei* that she should be taking the trash out, etc. Akahana had already assimilated into her American lifestyle; so it took her mother's prompting to remind her of her Japanese cultural background, i.e. her duties, given her place in the family.

As a result of being at the extreme end of High Context culture, the Japanese are often misperceived and underestimated. Americans might believe they lack initiative, since the expectation is for the Japanese person to speak up and "tell it to me straight."

American to Germany:

"It's very true that Americans often loosely say 'oh we should get together sometime' whereas here people take that very literally and I found someone at my doorstep because I had said we should go out. Lesson quickly learned."

LOW CONTEXT

The Swiss Germans are at the Low end of Low Context communication. As a result, Swiss Germans have been the butt of jokes and have experienced misperceptions. For example, Americans have found it "rude" when a complete Swiss German stranger tells them to "Lock the car," or, "You put the trash out incorrectly." Americans perceive the comments as mandates, orders, or judgments made against them as opposed to assistance or helpful information.

It is very difficult for those who are Low Context/Direct to understand how they may come across as rude or unkind. One attractive, blonde German executive in her early 30's came to California and shared with me her perception of American men as being aggressive. I explained that "aggressive" is a label; so if she could please describe the behavior. She said that she was rollerblading on the bike path at the beach and there were a handful of guys in beach chairs people-watching. As she started to skate by, one of them called out to her, "Hey! Why don't you come over here and talk to me? I think you are cute." Hearing the statement as a question, the German responded, "No, I will not go over and talk to you, because I do not think you are cute." After I told her that his ego was probably bruised, she proceeded to logically explain how her comment is not insulting because lack of attraction is a fact of life. Not everyone likes the same flavor! This response to the described scenario makes complete sense to other Germans, while Americans laugh or cringe at the story. An American response might be to simply smile, wave, do nothing, or say hello and keep going.

Genders are often split into High and Low Context. An example of a Male (Low Context) comment: "Ask for what you want. Let us be clear on this one: Subtle hints do not work! Strong hints do not work! Obvious hints do not work! Just say it!"

Dutchman to USA:

"What I have noticed is that the boss is really the boss here. In the Netherlands your manager normally talks to you before you are assigned a new role or task. I got a role assigned that I didn't feel would be right for me. When I confronted him with that, he looked very surprised. He did not expect any pushback. I explained him my side of the story and specifically why I thought the job was not right for me, not such a good career move, etc. In the end he turned his decision around and assigned someone else and I got the role that I wanted. Later he told me that I was probably right in speaking up, but he also told me that other US managers could take it differently."

High Context Gender (information is Implicit and Indirect) ↓

Women

Men

Low Context Gender (information is Explicit and Direct) ↑

Women are at the High end. While we are all familiar with several women who do not hold back, this book is focusing on broad generalizations. This is not an attempt to categorize women into all being High Context/Indirect communicators. We have too many examples to suggest that is not the case. However, around the world, most women relative to their national male counterparts can be categorized as being *more* High Context/Indirect.

Those who come from more indirect cultures often have the psycho-emotional barrier of being "rude" to state things so directly because their values usually entail Harmony, Collectivism, and Relationship Orientation. They hope that you can "read between the lines" because it sounds more delicate to do so. They don't want to have to break it down to you...you "should just know!" However, anytime "should" or "supposed to" is used, a value preference of the speaker is revealed. Conversely, if you come from a more direct culture, and someone from a more Indirect, Harmony, Collectivism, and Relationship Orientation culture asks you a personal question (for example, in Libya, one might ask you how much money you make), and you prefer to not disclose such information, you respond without answering -- which means that you talk, in general, about the subject of money.

Korea, like many Asian countries, is receiver-oriented (a feminine style of communication): The listener makes sense of what is being said. Note that this style works only when the listener is capable of paying close attention.

Here is an example from Malcolm Gladwell's book *Outliers* (pp. 216-217):

Division Chief: It's cold and I'm kind of hungry.

[MEANING: Why don't you buy a drink or something to eat?]

Employee: How about having a glass of liquor?

[MEANING: I will buy liquor for you.]

Division Chief: It's okay. Don't bother.

[MEANING: I will accept your offer if you repeat it.]

Employee: You must be hungry. How about going out?

[MEANING: I insist upon treating you.]

Division Chief: Shall I do so?

[MEANING: I accept.]

Those who come from more direct cultures often have extreme difficulty circumventing the issue so that you can receive it with kid gloves. They are not accustomed to speaking in a roundabout fashion, and have difficulty in doing so, because their values usually entail fixed time, confrontation, and task orientation. If you ask them a closed-ended question (expecting a "yes" or "no" answer), then you will get a "yes" or "no" answer; not a socially graceful one.

The conflict between High/Low Context and Direct/Indirect Communication can lead to hurt feelings. One Mexican executive told me that he informed his wife that if she is to work in the United States, she needs to leave her feelings in the car – meaning: when you park the car, don't take the emotional, sensitive part of you into work because it is all about work.

Here are some examples of Direct/Indirect communication. One tip to diagnose a comment as Direct is: Is the statement *telling* you what to do? Or, it is probably Indirect if you can say "yes" to: Is the statement more *informational*?

1.   I wrote a to-do list and posted it on the fridge.
2.   We are managing our inventory the best we can.
3.   It's trash night.
4.   I think I heard there is a new restaurant in town.
5.   This information would be most useful because the project is scheduled for launch in early May.

The answer to these five statements is that all of them are informational. They are indirect statements. They were made with the intent to motivate you to pick up on the hint that once you hear the information, you will seize the baton, and carry it forward. Of course, this would most likely work if you share the values of Indirect- and High Context communication, Collectivism, and Relationship Orientation. If not, no one has *told* you what they would like for you to do, so you might think that they are merely speaking aloud.

Here are the same statements said in Direct communication style:

1. I wrote a to-do list and posted it on the fridge. = Your to-do list in posted on the fridge.

2. We are managing our inventory the best we can. = Please assist us in managing our inventory.

3. It's trash night. = Eddie, please take out the trash.

4. I think I heard there is a new restaurant in town. = Let's go to Koi tonight.

5. This information would be most useful because the project is scheduled for launch in early May. = I need this information by noon this Friday to stay on target for our project launch. Will you please send it to me by noon Friday?

Certain professions require more High Context skill; others are more Low Context.

High Context Professions (information is Implicit and Indirect) ↓

Human Resources

Marketing/Sales

Management

Manufacturing Products

Research & Development

Technical

Information Systems

Engineers

Finance

Low Context Professions (information is Explicit and Direct) ↑

Note how those professions on the High end tend to be more Right Brain. These professions tend to rely on qualitative data and intuition. The focus is on the "soft," or more appropriately put, Behavioral Sciences. Right Brain people tend to be more creative in seeking alternate approaches. The right brain is non-verbal and uses imagery. Therefore, "Right Brains" tend to be visual learners. Incidentally, Human Resources is a field dominated by women. Interestingly, while imagery can get right-brained people excited, they are known for being more "turned on" by words. For example, the famous play Cyrano de Bergerac is about a woman who falls in love with a man because of the words he so poetically gifts her. Modern-day examples could be non-famous, not wealthy musicians – their musical abilities make them alluring.

The professions on the Low end tend to be more Left Brain. These professions tend to rely more on quantitative data and proven facts. The focus is on the hard sciences. Left Brain people tend to be more linear in their approaches. The left brain is non-verbal and rational; it tends to reduce thoughts to numbers and words. Therefore, "Left Brains" tend to be auditory learners. And incidentally, Finance – a quantitative field - is a field dominated by men. Interestingly, while words can get them excited, they are known for being more "turned on" by imagery. I'm guessing examples are unnecessary here.

CHAPTER 11

TOOLS

The first tool is the **Cultural Iceberg**. Understand the values that make-up your iceberg. Sometimes all you need is comprehension to work on the issues that press your triggers. About 88% of an iceberg is beneath the waterline. Much like culture, the little piece you do see is what we call Explicit Culture. **Explicit Culture** includes the aspects of culture that you can *see* (items or behavior) or *hear* (sounds or words). Beneath the waterline is Implicit Culture. **Implicit Culture** includes at the base Values and Beliefs that rise towards the surface in the form of Assumptions before manifesting into Explicit Culture.

An incident that occurred with one of my clients is that her boss called her into his office. Upon entering, he beckoned her to have a seat. His feet were up on his desk. Knowing that her culture (Chinese[24]) finds this behavior to be offensive, I move to her Interpretation. She says that her boss' behavior means that he thinks she is a peon and is showing her what he thinks of her by showing her the soles of his shoes. I then move to Expectations. She said that a "proper" boss would sit up straight (with the bottom of his spine to the back of the chair) and have his hands folded on his desk when she entered.

These Interpretations and Expectations exposed her Values to me. She had in mind an expected type of sitting protocol (Formality).

---

[24] Feet up on desk is offensive from the Middle East – which is considered part of Asia – to the rest of Asia.

She mentioned her awareness of their roles in the org chart of boss/subordinate (Hierarchy), interpreted that he was displaying an unspoken message (Indirect/High Context), and yet the surprise of it demonstrated his apparent inability to understand the expected team dynamics (Group).

However, Americans do not come from a Formal, Hierarchical, Indirect, Group-oriented culture; hence, culture shock was the result. Americans, in relation to the Chinese, are Informal, Equality-oriented, Direct, and Individualistic.

An American at His Desk

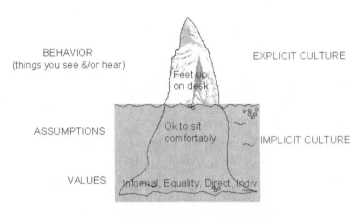

Chinese Encountering an American

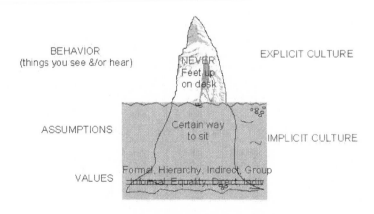

The second tool is **DIE**. Description. Interpretation. Expectation. This is just a verbal way of doing the cultural iceberg. Cultural Anthropologists agree that the best way to immerse yourself into a culture is to be a participant-observer. If there is some behavior that you do not understand or someone's behavior has gotten you all riled up, follow the DIE acronym. For example, "You've been late six times in the last two weeks." (Description/Observation). "I'd like to hear from you how you interpret that behavior (seeking Interpretation), because I start to think that you're trying to work as little as possible." (offering Interpretation). "I want you to be late no more than once a month." (Expectation) Check for understanding and follow-up.

Sharing the observation is a gift of feedback. It provides meaning to the recipient of your words, and it also adds meaning to the behavior for you. It is entirely different to take the same situation and contaminate the communication with a value judgment/thought. For example, "I know what your problem is, you like to get paid but you don't like to work."

American to Japan:

"One thing that stands out as very different is that the feedback I get (or lack of feedback) from my bosses and co-workers is non-existent. Maybe my work environment in the US was exceptional but I was getting regular feedback as to my performance and progress. Here in the last 6 months, I've heard only 2 words of encouragement from my boss, 'Good job,' after just one of my assignments. He probably doesn't realize how important those two words were to me. I still can hear them ringing in my ears even as I write to you now. I guess no news here is good news. My motto at home was, 'no news is never good news.'"

The **Ladder of Inference** is a model created by Peter Senge. It demonstrates the steps we take from our first observation to actions or inferences we make based on an observation. The model follows that we make an observation, select data from that observation, and climb up the rungs toward meaning, assumptions, conclusions, and, ultimately, beliefs. All that climbing usually stems from our own Cultural Baggage. The best way we can discover the true meaning is by asking questions. Many times, we quickly rise up the ladder in that knee-jerk reaction to get to a conclusion or belief that we are certain is true, when, in reality, it is applied meaning.

When the talented Italian opera singer Andrea Bocelli delivered his first performance in New York City, a critic wrote something along the lines of, Bocelli's magnificence has clearly gone to his head as he failed to establish eye contact with his adoring audience. The critic had risen up the Ladder of Inference (see image below) by first **selecting** from the observable data the fact (or behavior) that Andrea did not establish eye contact. This part no one can dispute.

The **meaning** he applied to the behavior is that lack of eye contact connotes snobbery and megalomania. The **assumption** he drew is that anyone who is talented (or, in other cases, intelligent, beautiful, etc.) feels s/he is at a higher level than the rest and, thus, does not need to look anyone in the eye. The **conclusion** is that Bocelli was "full of himself" because he is such a fantastic singer that this clear talent gives him justification to act as though he is better than the rest. The critic's **belief** is that Bocelli's personality is a detriment to his talent. The **action** he took was to write a negative review on Bocelli. If you know anything about Andrea Bocelli, you would then know that he is blind. Blind people have a considerable challenge to look anyone in the eye.

I once had an Englishwoman leave California for her first visit to New York City. She asked me to prep her for what she should expect culturally, and she returned to share that she had experienced exactly what I had told her. I wondered, which part? She said that she had gotten off the subway, and a very well-dressed man bumped into her roughly. Normally, the meaning she would have applied would have been the classic "New Yorkers are rude." Instead of racing up the Ladder of Inference, she remembered that I said New Yorkers may not stop to apologize for bumps because the sheer number of people bustling throughout the city makes it a frequent occurrence, especially in a place where everything needs to happen in a "New York minute."

We could even refer to the Ladder of Inference as **Othello's Error**. In Shakespeare's Othello, Othello observed an emotion from his beloved wife Desdemona that he mistakenly interpreted as *fear of being caught* as opposed to *fear of being punished*. He believed that he had been cuckolded by her; yet, he was not. Othello did not practice inquiry nor did he consider alternative reasons as to why Desdemona showed fear. He falsely interpreted, or inferred, her demeanor as a validation to his suspicions.

Desdemona: Alas, he (my friend) is betrayed and I undone!

Othello: Out, strumpet! Weep'st thou for him to my face?

Desdemona: O, banish me, my lord, but kill me not!

Othello: Down, strumpet!

The third tool is **Active Listening**. Active Listening is listening for meaning. The attention is focused on the speaker. Judgment is suspended. People are usually thinking about how they are going to respond or are perhaps distracted by their emotions to be fully attentive. Active Listening entails observation of the speaker's body language and behavior. If it is just *words* that are your observation, paraphrasing for understanding is key. The speaker desires to be understood. If *emotions* are observed, you might wish to address the underlying emotion. For example, "You seem frustrated, is that because...?" One is *not* practicing Active Listening by making a defensive comment such as, "That's not true!" The message between the lines/words here, or **metamessage**, is "I'm more interested in defending myself than I am in investigating the complexities of what might be going on for me in our relationship." A healthier message is, "So you're saying that you prefer more direct guidance from me as a manager?" Consider the dialogues below.

Employee Not Practicing Active Listening – Culture Clash

Boss:	It looks like we're going to require you to come in on Saturday.
Employee:	I see.
Boss:	Can you come in on Saturday?
Employee:	Yes, I think so. (sign of indefinite commitment)
Boss:	That'll be a great help.
Employee:	Yes. Saturday's a special day, did you know? (indirect communication)
Boss:	How do you mean?
Employee:	It's my grandfather's 80th birthday. (disclosing values)
Boss:	How nice. I hope you all enjoy it very much.
Employee:	Thank you. I appreciate your understanding. (believes metamessage is received).

Employee Practicing Active Listening[25] – Cultural Alignment

Boss:	You're so quiet during meetings, and then over lunch you come up with these incredible marketing strategies.
Employee:	You're saying that I don't talk enough during meetings. (voice tone downwards – downwards connotes comprehension; not inquiry)
Boss:	Well, you know, the whole reason for these meetings is for everyone to get their opinion out there so that we can make an informed decision.
Employee:	You think that I should let everyone know what I think during the meeting, not after. (voice tone downwards)
Boss:	Yeah, like last week, you knew Bob was wrong, but you didn't say anything until we met for lunch on Thursday. You could have saved everyone hours if you had shared your thoughts at Monday's meeting.
Employee:	So what can I do to be more effective at next week's meeting? (genuine question: voice tone upwards)
Boss:	You should let people know what you think, even if you disagree with them. There's nothing wrong with disagreeing. It keeps everyone on their toes.

---

[25] Adapted from Cornelius Grove & Associates manual.

The fourth tool is **Contribution Recognition.** Not recognizing what you have contributed to a tense situation may lead you to say something like, "No, I had good intentions." Your metamessage here is that you do not wish to be judged inaccurately. Remember, blame is about *judging*; contribution is about *understanding*. Taking responsibility for your contribution sounds more like, "There are a number of things I've done that have made this situation harder..."

CHAPTER 12

PRESENTATION STYLE DIFFERENCES

There are two major stylistic differences when it comes to presentation, i.e. speech: Inductive and Deductive. Inductive speech is what is most rewarded by Americans. **Inductive** speech is presenting the conclusion first, and may entail more information. **Deductive** speech is presenting the background first (history, methodology, context, etc), and proceeds in the direction of the conclusion.

American to Puerto Rico (part of the USA):

"I learned don't ever get into a discussion about politics or religion, and to allow people the time to get the story out - you cannot go straight to the point."

Many Europeans laugh at American PowerPoint presentations because they are inductive. Inductive presentations often incorporate bullet points. They may leap to the next subject if no questions are asked. For example, "We found that this product tested 99.98% for safety." If no one questioned as to how that statistic came to be, the next subject might be discussed on the next slide.

Men tend to be Inductive conversationalists. They believe that Yes and No are perfectly acceptable answers to almost every question. Hence, a Deductive conversationalist may have the perception that the Inductive speaker is not really interested in a conversation. In fact, they may feel like it's akin to "pulling teeth" to get a conversation going. Consider the following conversation:

Arlene: Where did you go last weekend?

Mike: Out.

Arlene: Where to?

Mike: Watsonville.

Arlene: What did you do?

Mike: Saw a movie.

Arlene: How was it?

Mike: Good.

Deductive listeners would prefer to hear the background first. An American listened patiently in a German boardroom as the session leader laid out the company history on the measure taken to ensure quality for its product. After about 50 minutes of methodology, the leader spent less than 10 minutes on the results. After the meeting, the American exclaimed, "Why didn't you spend time focusing on results?!" To which the German replied, "The method *is* the results." There is a line of reasoning to be followed in the deductive approach; whereas, one does not appear to exist with the inductive approach.

Another Deductive example happened when I was in the home of a Mexican-American family. The teenage son explained, "Dad, I'm going to go over to Conner's house to study for a test tomorrow, and then we're going to practice some basketball for the big game on Saturday night. May I please have the keys to the Ford?" Inductive would have been, "Dad, may I please have the keys to the Ford?" Dad would toss him the keys and/or ask, "What for?"

Women tend to be Deductive conversationalists. They believe that if they share the entire story, you get a better sense of understanding. An Inductive conversationalist may lament ever having asked the question; and, on one occasion, actually said to a Deductive conversationalist, "God gave you two ears and one mouth for a reason!" Using the aforementioned situation spun around, consider the following:

Mike: What did you do last weekend?

Arlene: I went into town with my friend Delia and we saw that new movie that just came out...you know the one with Robert Downey, Jr. Boy, do I love him...Iron Man. You need to make sure that you see it in surround sound, because it is filled with action! We had a great time.

Inductive   **Deductive**

Prefers the summary point at the start,   Prefers the background information
Followed by supporting data   at the start, followed by analysis and
                                                 conclusions.

MONOCHRONIC/ POLYCHRONIC

Chronemics is the application of time in culture. The root of the word, "Chron," stems from "chronos" which comes from Greek, meaning "time." "Mono" means one, as in "monogamous" or "monotheistic." "Poly" means more than one, as in "polygamous" or "polytheistic." So, as compound words we are referring to "one thing at a time" being **Monochronic**; and, "multiple things at a time" being **Polychronic**. Culturally, Americans have been known for behaving and speaking in monochronic fashion; however, with the advent of technology, younger American behavior and speech has become much more Polychronic.

Less than a couple of decades ago, American behavior was very Monochronic. For example, all messages were held until after a meeting. If it was urgent, an admin[26] might slip into a meeting to deliver a pink slip to alert you to the issue. Today, we are reached directly by cellular phone text messaging and Instant Messaging (IM) via computer. Phone calls were linear because there was no Caller ID or Call Waiting. My sister used to be highly insulted by my answering Call Waiting – which I did because I shared the line with two housemates. She argued at how rude it was for me to "make" her wait; that is, until she married and currently never hesitates to place me on Call Waiting. Your environment shapes your culture. This is called **Social Cognitive Theory** – who you socialize with and/or where you socialize alters the way you think and feel. Who or what in your environment shapes how you communicate?

Monochronic speech is still widely practiced in the USA, except for those who enjoy debate – usually those in law or politics (power play fields). We take turns speaking and generally do not appreciate interruptions or interjections.

Polychronic people get bored with Monochronic communications. They are accustomed to overlapping speech. They do not see that style as an interruption; rather, it is an enhancer. They wish to illustrate that they follow where you are going. Often these enhancers include the following: "You don't say!" "Wow," "Hmmm," etc. For Polychronic speakers, to have only one person speak at a time is like watching junior league tennis...slowly the ball goes back over the net. They may wish to engage in a conversation with you, possibly even on a separate topic, while you are already conversing with someone else. This is

---

[26] Formerly referred to as "secretary," which is now an antiquated term.

common in the Middle East and Latin America. They are equally adept at listening to two entirely different conversations as well.

Behaviorally, Polychronic people feel most productive when they are multi-tasking. One Mexican financial analyst was asked by his American boss why he had so many spreadsheets open at the same time. It is because he feels capable of working on several simultaneously! Many people who wait tables or act as corporate receptionists are often Polychronic – they are comfortable with many variables occurring at the same time. For example, while Monochronic mainland Americans find that a quiet office is conducive for task completion, Polychronic Puerto Ricans would find their workplace utterly boring without music being played for all to enjoy. This begs the question...

Can Listening to Music Help Us Work Better?[27]

According to a report in the journal Neuroscience of Behavior and Physiology, the Russian Academy of Sciences discovered that a person's ability to recognize visual images, including letters and numbers, is faster when either rock or <u>classical music</u> is playing in the background.

If you are aiming to be more productive through being more relaxed, then you may be interested to learn that research has shown that music with an upbeat rhythm can reduce stress hormone levels by as much as 41%.

Some of the most publicized studies into whether <u>listening to music</u> increases productivity have centered on what has been termed the "Mozart effect." The term got its name after a study showed that college students had performed better

---

[27] Article by Mike Seddon, www.articlesbase.com, Posted: Oct 30th, 2006

solving mathematical problems when listening to classical music. The effect of listening to Mozart does not appear to be limited to humans either. Apparently cows will produce more milk if Mozart is played.

CHAPTER 13

VALUES

"I can endure any how if I have a why." – Friedrich Nietzsche

Values leads directly to behavior &/or speech. We start learning our values at about age 2. Values come from our parents, generally. By age 5, we can see the child's personality emerging. At age 10, the values that a child has learned are embedded. It is at this stage, that a child tends to form a group identity away from the family. It is increasingly difficult to separate a child from his/her friends between ages 10-14; especially, in my personal and professional experience, girls. Between the ages 10-25, there is much room for developing acceptance and tolerance which is granted usually with cultural exposure.

Age 25 is a very important year for brain development. The last part of the brain to develop is the prefrontal cortex, which finishes development at around age 25. It is the part that deals with weighing consequences of one's actions. Consequently, corporations adopt risk-averse strategies based on the statistics which correlate directly with prefrontal cortex development. Notice, for example, how many car rental agencies will not rent cars to anyone under age 26. Also, divorce statistics are higher for those under age 26. And, in 2005, the French government was trying to pass a law that would allow corporations to "make redundant" (i.e. fire) anyone under age 26 –

since the current law made it difficult to do so. Huge protests of discrimination resulted.

Once past age 25, a person's values are set. You are who you are, and there is room for depth and maturity – you just have your value preferences set to where you like them. Interestingly, my research indicates that a regression to core values can be triggered at specific times in a person's life: 1) a life-altering event (e.g. September 11, 2001), 2) mid-life crisis (generally a feeling of despair of something not experienced fully), 3) old age (definitively the case with all in the most elderly group). Geriatric people wish to return to a happy time, with most happy times occurring typically before age 26. If English is a second language, there is regression to the first language. English may be understood, but the native first language is commonly spoken.

Americans can be generalized as having a core set of values; however, just as with anywhere, there are regional differences. Note how different the West (e.g. California), newer history- Cowboys and proximity to Mexico & arguably Asia, can be from the East (e.g. New York), older history- industrial epicenter and proximity to Europe.

CALIFORNIA	NEW YORK	OVERALL
Collectivistic	Individualistic	Individualistic
Relationship	Task	Task
Indirect	Direct	Direct
Informal	Formal	Informal
Egalitarian	Hierarchical	Egalitarian

Expressive	Instrumental	Instrumental
Change	Tradition	Change
Fluid Time	Fixed Time	Fixed Time

There are more values than what I present here; however, after this list, the values may seem too similar to differentiate. The difficulty of value differences varies for each individual; generally speaking, most Americans tend to experience the most difficulty with these values: Collectivism, Indirect and High Context Communication, and Relationship/Process-Orientation.

These are the values I will cover in the chapters that follow:

Direct*[28] ....Indirect
Low Context* ....High Context
Inductive* ....Deductive
Monochronic*..............Polychronic

Individualism*...Collectivism/Group
Task* ....Relationship/Process
Confrontation*...Harmony
Informal*...Formal
Control over Environment* ....Fate/Destiny
Instrumental*..Expressive
Change* ....Tradition
Fixed Time* ....Fluid Time
Equal*...Hierarchy
Private Space*..Public Space
Competition* ....Cooperation
Present-Future* ....Past-orientation

[28] The asterisks represent where the USA, as a whole, stands with *most* other countries. Again, it is relative.

Practical/Pragmatic/Efficiency*..................Idealism

Materialism*..Spiritualism

Doing*..Being

Universalism*...Particularism

Tolerance for Ambiguity/Risk-Takers*...........Need for Certainty/Risk-Averse

CHAPTER 14

INDIVIDUALISM/COLLECTIVISM (GROUP)

"The sweetest sound to a man's ear is the sound of his own name." – Mark Twain

One way to quickly ascertain whether someone comes from an Individualistic culture or a Collective culture is by his/her name. This is not foolproof, however, it does provide much insight. Take, for example, the following two people who gave birth to the former President of Mexico:

Luis Calderón Vega

María del Carmen Hinojosa González

Felipe de Jesús Calderón Hinojosa

In most Spanish-speaking cultures, a person has two last names. The first last name is paternal, stemming from the father. The second last name is maternal, stemming from the mother. Both families are acknowledged to show a union. When the woman marries, she retains those two last names and adds "de" plus the husband's paternal name. In the above example, if Felipe's hypothetical sister Lucia were to marry Juan Antonio García Monzon, she then becomes Lucia (plus any additional first names) Calderón Hinojosa de García.

Many feminists oppose the addition of the "de" when incorporating the husband's name because they feel it connotes "possession." Remember, the objective of the name is to define from which two families you are biologically related and to which other you are also, by marriage, "of," "from," "belong," or "pertain to." You are "in the circle."

Chinese names also illustrate the value of the Collective. Chinese names begin with the family name, then the generational name, and a given name. For example, Hu Jintao/Jin-Tao/Jin Tao (the generational name and given name can be compounded together, joined by a hyphen, or separated).

When a Chinese woman marries, she does not change her name. She just adds the status title of being married with "Madame" to her last name – which appears first.

Liu Yonqing (Madame Liu), for example.

In the Middle East, some more cultural and linguistic knowledge is necessary to notice the Collective nature. You can tell who the father of someone is named by hearing "bin" (a.k.a. ibn) – meaning "son of." For example, the King of Bahrain is Shaikh (a title given to clergy or members of the royal family) Hamad bin Isa Al Khalifa. So who's his daddy? Answer: Isa. His father's full name is Shaikh Isa bin Hamad Al Khalifa. Notice how the current king has his grandfather's name; likewise, the king will pass along his father's name Isa to his son, and so on. Also commonly used to reflect the pride of family is usage of "Abu" – meaning "father of." So, in the abovementioned example, the Bahraini King could also be referred to affectionately as "Abu Isa."

TEST: What is the first name of Osama bin Laden's father?

Answer: Laden

To add a title of "Mr." to the name, it is *neither* Mr. Laden nor Mr. bin Laden, rather Mr. Osama.

Individualism is the focus of people on themselves (and their nuclear family). Men tend to be Individualists. An example of personal accomplishment as a sign of Individualism is, "Christopher Columbus did not need directions and neither do we." The common perception by Collectivists is that Individualists are selfish and uncaring. Here are some differentiators for those who are of Individualistic cultures:

- Say "I" a lot.
- Hold opinions; speak openly (can be confrontational).
- Identity is based on the individual. E.g. "Hi, I'm John Doe, call me John."
- Guilt (e.g. Protestants)
- Tend to apply Universal value-standard
- Task-oriented
- Promotions are based on merit
- Management expects initiative and a proactive nature by employee

Group/Collectivism has the focus on those circles to which you belong (e.g. families, organizations, alumni groups, etc.). These circles support you in exchange for loyalty. They are clannish (e.g. the infamous Hatfields and McCoys in the South). The common perception by Individualists of Collectivists is that they are family-oriented and can be exclusive. As such, it would be wise for Individualists to refrain from sharing "Jerry Springer"-type of familial information, such as being estranged from siblings or disputes with parents/in-laws.

<u>American to Brazil:</u>

"My photo album was a big hit. I highly recommend it to your future clients. I had about a dozen photos of my family and about eight of my staff and laboratories. People eagerly looked at the photos and it seemed to have improved the connection. I usually brought it out after a half hour or hour of general discussions."

Here are some differentiators for those who are of Collectivistic cultures:

- Say "We" a lot
- Value opinions of the group; maintain harmony
- Identity is based on the social network
- Shame (e.g. Catholics)
- Tend to apply Particularistic value-standards
- Relationship-oriented
- Promotions take employee's "in-group" into account.
- Management expects that employees value their constant supervision

Arab Maxim:

"I am with my brother against my cousin. I am with my cousin against a stranger."

Affiliating with a group creates a sense of identity and security. From sororities/fraternities to religious organizations and so on, people vary in their degree of Collectivism. *Umma* is the collective spirit of brotherhood in Islam. Gordon Thomas, author of several books on intelligence agencies, writes of how Meir Amit created the *sayanim* (volunteer Jewish helpers). Amit knew that despite one's nationality, each *sayan* recognizes a greater loyalty to protect Israel from its enemies. These *sayans* provide assistance to the cause with no questions asked.

If you understand the values, you don't need a list of do's and don'ts. For example, we've already established the Japanese are Collectivistic. They have concerns for the group. So, why would someone from a Collectivistic culture wear a surgical mask? Answer: They are not necessarily germaphobes...they do not want to infect *others* with their cold! Here's another: If you remember the big boom boxes of the late '70's/ early '80's, why did Sony invent the Walkman[29]? Most Americans believe it's because that way others could not disturb us with their music as we listened to ours. That is the Individualistic point of view. Consider the Particularistic point of view. Answer: Sony invented the Walkman so that users would not disturb *others* with their music.

---

[29] The Walkman was a portable device that allowed one to listen to cassette tapes through headphones.

CHAPTER 15

TASK/RELATIONSHIP (PROCESS)

Task is the focus placed on what you wish to accomplish. The common perception by Relationship-oriented cultures of Task-oriented cultures is that they are unsympathetic and workaholics. Men tend to be more Task-oriented. They have been known to make comments such as, "Come to us with a problem <u>only</u> if you want help solving it. That's what we do. Sympathy is what your girlfriends are for."

<u>Englishman to USA</u>:

"I bought a plaque from the Ronald Reagan Museum that says, 'Just do it!' Apparently, it's something he had on his desk in the Oval Office. It's something that I admire about Americans, although it does seem a bit rushed at times."

Since most American managers believe that "time is money," let's examine the Project Manager's Pyramid. The **Project Manager's Pyramid** holds the premise that a manager can only have two of the following variables at any time, and the third suffers as a result: Quality (Q), Time (T), Cost ($).

If Americans choose T and $, Q suffers. From this approach, spring the jokes about Made in America as meaning "having low quality." For countries where Q is paramount, such as Switzerland or Japan, they will make a choice as to whether they would like to have it quickly, thus pay more (T + Q); OR, they would like to pay less, and can afford to wait (Q + $).

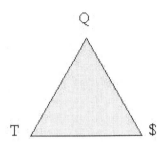

<u>American to Switzerland</u>:

"The Swiss are NOT motivated by money. I'm not sure what motivates them. Getting services established is like pulling teeth. 1 month for internet, I offered $500 to speed up the process but they wouldn't take it. Cell phone technical support is at best 48hr call back, at worst 1 month to resolve. Generally, they could care less about servicing the client. I had a cell phone sales person who was helping me troubleshoot just leave to go to lunch while the problem still existed. I wanted to cancel my service contract on the spot. I still might. I'm now in direct contact with the head of customer relations to get that problem resolved.

Registering with the commune can be trying. It took 7 trips to get that cleared up. I scheduled a meeting with the head of their office and he refused to see me citing no excuse. Needless to say, I wrote a formal complaint to the head of the commune citing his irresponsibility and his office's.

Food is insanely expensive. $50 (USD) per lb for steaks. $12 (USD) per gallon for milk. Makes LA look cheap. This fire is fed by high international tariffs on food goods to protect Swiss business. I've heard rumor that it's as high as 75%.

Forget shipping products here, they open every package in the mail. Then value it, and send the recipient a bill.

The 3 mo's psychological roller coaster is definitely real."

Relationship-orientation is the focus placed on maintaining and establishing strong social networks. Women tend to be more Relationship-oriented. People from these cultures want to know that the friendship they extend to you is there for the long haul. My advice is to never say that you are on an assignment for 2-3 years; you are there for however long it takes because you enjoy the people so much (make it something honest, be authentic). The common perception by Task-oriented cultures of Relationship-oriented cultures is that they are friendly and waste time and/or don't prioritize.

Here are a couple of statements from Relationship-oriented executives:

- "The only way you can learn is by being there. Make 1-2 trips to the region yearly."

- "My solution to almost everything is: Let's get together and talk. The only way you can do that is to physically be in a room and talk."

Dutch (Task) to USA:

"It doesn't make sense to make friends with anyone here. We're only here for 18 months."

The Swiss Germans are known for being the most Process-oriented in the world. They believe in *Ordnung* -- that is, "Process." In their opinion, there is one way to do things correctly and over the centuries they have perfected the process. They are proud when people quip that the Swiss trains are so punctual, you can set your watch to the train schedule. In fact, they have Horological Museums (Horology is the science of time) that display clocks, watches, and other timekeeping artifacts which still hold perfect time, despite being hundreds of years old.

American to Switzerland:

"Here's our recycling area, as you can tell it's a bit extensive. On the back row from the left, you have the caps from the coffee cups in 1, PET - is plastic, to the right of that is aluminum, and after that is biodegradable. The front row, you have batteries on the very left, white glass, colored glass and 2 containers of paper and carton."

Dominican (Relationship) to USA:

"These people who work around me in cubicles have had their desks for years and they don't know each other. I've only been here for weeks and I've introduced them!"

Cultural tendencies of Task/Relationship Orientations:

Task-Oriented	Relationship-Oriented
Yes = Yes	Yes = Yes / No / "I want you to think yes."
Direct	Indirect
Brief, to the point	Elaborate, circular
Informal	Formal
Egalitarian	Hierarchical
Explicit (Low Context)	Implicit (High Context)
Results-oriented	Process-oriented
Information sharing	Information withholding
Sequential	Intermittent (boss there) Simultaneous (colleagues)

People who come from Relationship-oriented cultures are more likely than Task-oriented cultures (which are more comfortable with trial & error) to prepare for their meetings learning about trivia and what they consider important pieces of information. Sometimes this entails learning the populations of cities/towns. I strongly recommend that, at a minimum, travelers be armed with the knowledge of WHO is the country leader, and WHERE the country is located. I once spoke with an American had just returned from a short assignment to Japan. When I asked her if she traveled to any of the other islands other than Honshū (where Tokyo is located), she responded, "I didn't go to *any* islands. I just stayed on the mainland." [30] Not knowing these simple pieces of information, needless to say, damages one's professional credibility.

I've put together the following quiz that involved all of the regional offices of a client company. What is most interesting for me to observe as a cultural analyst is to see whether the group works independently or collectively, competitively or cooperatively, etc. Try and guess the country answer for each number listed below.

INTERNATIONAL TRIVIA QUIZ

1. Which country has as its Government's Official Credo: the "3-S Plan" of Social Responsibility, Social Attitude, and Skill?

2. We're the "real" Down Under.

3. We have four official languages: French, Italian, German, and Romansch. English is the fifth, unofficial language.

4. We did *not* invent the hamburger, french fries, or pizza; but we sure made it popular.

5. We speak Strine.

6. A side-to-side toss of one's head indicates agreement. The up-and-down head nod means "no."

7. We're North Americans, too.

8. You are not automatically of our *nationality*, just because you were born here.

9. Don't be afraid if a stranger approaches you and wants to chat.

---

[30] Japan largely consists of four main islands, namely: Honshū, Hokkaidō, Kyūshū, and Shikoku.

10. We suffer from the Brain Drain. We will not become the 51st State.

11. We're Kiwis; not Aussies.

12. Although we're in South America, we are not Hispanic.

13. Don't trail off when you speak with us...The most important word in a sentence is usually the final one.

14. We hold the distinction of having Europe's oldest university, founded in Bologna in the 12th Century.

15. Please do not distribute your business cards like cards in a game of Poker. Practice the *Meishi* before you come.

16. We are the world's oldest continuous civilization.

17. We are also known as *Hispaniola*.

18. The custom of "les bises" originated in our country.

19. This country's flag is also known as the Saltire. It is said to be one of the oldest national flags of any country, dating back at least to the 12th century.

20. Cartographers mixed up the name of our capital with the name of our territory.

   If you are working with a company regional office, *you must be aware of what the regional office's flag looks like.*

Answers to Int'l Trivia Quiz

Answers continued:

1. Which country has as its Government's Official Credo: the "3-S Plan" of Social Responsibility, Social Attitude, and Skill? **Singapore.**

2. We're the "real" Down Under. **Netherlands.**[31]

3. We have four official languages: French, Italian, German, and Romansch. English is the fifth, unofficial language. **Switzerland.**[32]

4. We did *not* invent the hamburger (Germany), french fries (Belgium), or pizza (Italy); but we sure made it popular. **USA.**

5. We speak Strine. **Australia.**[33]

---

[31] Often mistaken for Holland (which is the equivalent of calling the USA after its largest state: Alaska), the Netherlands means "below land" and was recovered from the water.

[32] Meanwhile, many Americans have complained at having to press "1" for English.

[33] Americans like to think we speak the same language as the Aussies and the British, but they both beg to differ.

6. A side-to-side toss of one's head indicates agreement. The up-and-down head nod means "no." **India.**

7. We're North Americans, too. **Mexico.**[34]

8. You are not automatically of our nationality, just because you were born here. **England.**[35]

9. Don't be afraid if a stranger approaches you and wants to chat. **Israel.**

10. We suffer from the Brain Drain. We will not become the 51st State. **Canada.**[36]

11. We're Kiwis; not Aussies. **New Zealand.**[37]

12. Although we're in South America, we are not Hispanic. **Brazil.**[38]

13. Don't trail off when you speak with us…The most important word in a sentence is usually the final one. **Germany.**[39]

14. We hold the distinction of having Europe's oldest university, founded in Bologna in the 12th Century. **Italy.**[40]

15. Please do not distribute your business cards like cards in a game of Poker. Practice the *Meishi* before you come. **Japan.**[41]

---

[34] Americans are notoriously bad at geography. I've had many Californians claim, "If Baja California doesn't belong to us, then why is it named Baja California?"

[35] This is a "trick" answer (see flag) because most people are familiar with the Union Jack which represents the United Kingdom.

[36] Canadians are not generally flattered when Americans say, "You are one of us!"

[37] Kiwis know it's hard for Americans to distinguish their accent from their more well-known neighbor, but they take offense at the mistake.

[38] Brazilians speak Portuguese because the history goes back to Portugal. Hispanic means the history goes back to Spain.

[39] Germans are known for being really good listeners for this reason.

[40] "Honest courtesans" created for themselves, as Simone de Beauvoir writes, "a situation almost equivalent to that of man... free in behavior and conversation," attaining, "the rarest intellectual liberty." For centuries courtesans enjoyed more power and independence than other women in Europe.

16. We are the world's oldest continuous civilization. **China.**[42]

17. We are also known as *Hispaniola*. **Dominican Republic.**

18. The custom of *"les bises"* originated in our country. **France.**

19. This country's flag is also known as the Saltire. It is said to be one of the oldest national flags of any country, dating back at least to the 12th century. **Scotland.**

20. Cartographers mixed up the name of our capital with the name of our territory. **Puerto Rico.**[43]

FRIENDSHIP AS THE PEACH

Friendship has been described using the metaphors of a peach and a coconut. Peaches are described as fuzzy on the outside, easy to penetrate, but suddenly there is a huge pit that does not allow for further penetration. While it's all relative, usually people from "colder" cultures tend to find Americans to be the peach if the perception is that Americans are friendly (fuzzy), open to starting relationships (e.g. have lunch together), but the relationship doesn't progress more. It's off to a quick start and then there's no further progression. This leads people from this culture to find "peaches" as superficial.

FRIENDSHIP AS THE COCONUT

Coconuts are described as rough on the outside (e.g. not a lot of smiles), difficult to penetrate (e.g. no social invites or small talk), but if one is persistent (or perhaps knows exactly where to strike), then the milk and "meat" is there to enjoy. Again, it is relative, people from

---

[41] Bring a special card case, leather or metallic. Present the card with two hands with the lettering facing your colleague. Make appreciable comments about your colleague's card, or at least read it!

[42] It is for this reason that many sociologists attribute the line, "The USA thinks in term of years; Europe in decades; and China in centuries."

[43] The capital was Puerto Rico (Rich Port). The island was San Juan (St. John).

"warmer" cultures tend to perceive Americans as unfriendly (rough), hard to get to know (who are they really?), but with time they discover a comfort zone (usually commonalities) and become friends.

My personal experience in Denmark was that the Danes (except for perhaps during the summer) are coconuts. They were not easy to get to know out in the Jutland.[44] One Texan from my language class left after 3 months (Culture Shock phase), because she couldn't handle how "unfriendly" the Danes are. I remember our instructor from the Faeroe Islands (isles owned by Denmark), explained to us after the Texan left that a Brazilian the previous year had expressed, "The Danes are difficult to get to know, but once you have one as a friend, you have one for life." That has indeed been my experience. If they give you their friendship, it is a loyal one which lasts indefinitely.

---

[44] Copenhagen, like most metropolitan areas, is more cosmopolitan and, therefore, is not "typically Danish."

CHAPTER 16

DIRECT (CONFRONTATION)/INDIRECT (HARMONY)

"Please nod your head up and down for when you say 'yes,' and shake your head from side to side for when you say 'yes,' so I can tell the difference." – Argentine to his Japanese colleague

Direct is the focus of speech being concise and precise. A common perception by Indirect cultures of Direct cultures is that they are rude and bossy. One of my former Korean clients told me that her German colleague is a supervisor who the others refer to as the "Nazi" behind her back, because of her direct manner in ascertaining whether work objectives have been met. Americans commonly say, "Don't beat around the bush," "What is the bottom line?" "What is the punchline?" and, "Give it to me straight."

Indirect is the focus of speech being diplomatic and harmonizing. The common perception by Direct cultures of Indirect cultures is that they are time-consuming and vague. One Mexican executive shared with me that she felt so "abandoned" by her supervisor that she decided to walk into his office and ask him what her job responsibilities were. Surprised, he walked her through the list of what she *already* knew. She was attempting to indirectly communicate to him that he hadn't *shown* her how to do the work; and, he presumed that since he himself had promoted her from Mexico, she already knew what to do!

Despite being known as direct, Americans are frequently misunderstood for saying, "How are you?" Even Australians, who come from the culture most similar to the American culture, have been known to stop and respond to the greeting as a question and are surprised to see Americans do not slow down for the answer. This situation is akin to the Malaysian[45] salutation, "Have you eaten?" Neither question is literal. The American does not want to hear about your details necessarily, and the Malaysian is not suggesting to buy you a meal. The greetings are phrased as questions with the message being "hello."

---

[45] This greeting is also common in other countries, e.g. Thailand, northern China, etc.

CHAPTER 17

LOW/HIGH CONTEXT

"Read my lips: no new taxes."
– George H. W. Bush, 1988 Republican National Convention

Low Context is the focus on words to convey meaning. Men tend to be Low Context. Men have been known to say, "If something we said can be interpreted two ways and one of the ways makes you sad or angry, we meant the other one," and, "If you ask a question you don't want an answer to, expect an answer you don't want to hear." The common perception by High Context cultures of Low Context cultures is that they leave out a lot of important/relevant details and, therefore, appear to not be interested in holding a real conversation.

High Context is when the focus is on how you say something rather than on what you actually say. Also, what one is *not* saying may be just as or more important as what one is saying. A common perception by Low Context cultures of High Context cultures is that they add superfluous details and, therefore, can be confusing, tedious, and boring.

CHAPTER 18

INFORMAL/FORMAL

"Sit up straight." – mom

Informal is the preference of a casual nature in dress, language, behavior, and posture. Americans and Australians rank the highest as the most informal cultures of the world. This stems from our common history in forming new countries in what was considered "wild territories" and the common wish to disassociate ourselves from the "condescending" British. A common perception by Formal cultures of Informal cultures is that they have no taste/etiquette/culture and are, therefore, uncouth.

Formal is the preference of a traditional nature in dress, language, behavior, and posture. Cultures that have a history of Royals pay a lot of attention to how these forms of explicit culture are handled. Consequently, most Formal cultures also are Hierarchical cultures, which breed a behavior of entitlement. Indeed, if the "correct" behaviors are not exhibited, there is much doubt to the validity or credibility of the executive being worthwhile. A common perception by Informal cultures of Formal cultures is that they are perhaps well-dressed, but may come across as aloof.

American to England:

"I met a few British women but most are busy with their jobs and families. I did make friends with my art teacher who has invited me to dinner parties and concerts. You were right about the British being more formal than Americans. Everything is planned months in advance and you have to take gifts and write thank you notes for everything.

I also joined the American Women's Club. This is a much more casual group. We get together to sew, go to the pubs, go shopping and do charity work. I am organizing a charity event next month at Christies Auction House. There are over 600 women in the American Women's Club and they are all educated, well traveled ladies."

<u>American to Japan:</u>

"I sat down at the conference table for our meeting. Then, one of my Japanese colleagues came in and asked me to sit in another chair. I remembered suddenly what you told me about the 'God-Seat' and the hierarchical order to seating, but he didn't know that I knew why he was moving me."

Linguistically, you will hear formality typically in the Hierarchical cultures. The word "you" varies. How the person addresses you depends on the relationship s/he has with you. German uses Sie/Du; Spanish uses Usted/Tú; French uses Vous/Tu. Either one can be a compliment or not, depending on the context. If you are a stranger or have a higher title or age, then the speaker who uses the formal "you" is attempting to signal respect. You also use the formal "you" to indicate that you have not developed intimacy yet and you are not within that inner circle. (Or, the speaker could just be formal with everyone). If you are a friend, the use of the informal "you" is to signal you have established intimacy. You also use the informal "you" to indicate that the other person is a stranger or has a lower title/age than you. Or, as in many parts of Spain, they are informal with everyone – which is called *tutear* (an infinitive verb which cannot be translated other than the following: to use the informal "you" when speaking with people).

FORMAL DINING

Since dining etiquette is vitally important to assert your credibility as an executive in Formal European cultures, it is necessary that you learn Continental Dining. **Continental Dining** is keeping the fork in the left hand and the knife in the right hand – never shall the twain change hands! This is imperative. Note that this is NOT important for Informal cultures, but we're not talking about what Informal cultures think. I once had a senior executive who, realizing that it's his cultural baggage, told me that despite working and living here in the States for 20 years, he still cringes when he sees an American eat "incorrectly" and immediately finds himself rating the executive as sub-par.

The historical origin of the American switching utensils while dining comes from the time of the Revolutionary War. Many British Loyalists had fled to Canada, but there were still several among the camps. Those who were Loyalists, or Red Coats themselves, were traditional in how they chose to eat the colonial food. Nothing was to be picked up with the hands. The revolutionary colonialists striving for independence decided to symbolically show their allegiance to America and not the British throne by deliberately switching utensils. This demonstrated to other revolutionary colonialists that they were on the same side. The custom has stayed with us to today. This story is not apocryphal!

Here is a list of important behaviors to remember when **dining worldwide**:

- Learn Continental Dining – this applies to pizza and open-faced sandwiches. Asia will be forgiving if you do not know how to use chopsticks.

- Wrists remain on the table; *not* on your lap. (This custom goes back to the time when this behavior demonstrated trust that dining companions would not pull a concealed weapon during the meal).

- Allow the host to offer the first toast.

- *Never* begin eating before the host, and try not to finish before the host.

- Remember "b" is for "bread" and "d" is for "drink." If you extend your index fingers, and curl the remaining three to form a circle with each respective thumb, the left hand will form a "b" and the right hand a "d." This is to remind you that your **b**read plate is on your left and your **d**rink is on your right. Sometimes the bread plates and glasses of your neighbors are placed quite close and you may mistakenly take the wrong plate/glass.

 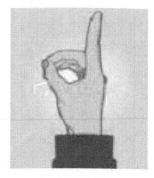

- Do NOT slurp your soup, except for in Asia where this is expected with soup and noodles.

- Remember to excuse yourself if you need to leave the table.

- The waiter will bring the bill when asked.

- The tip is usually included even though it is not obvious. Leaving 5% is equivalent to giving 20% here.

- Never say, "I'll pay you back." It is not about money; rather, friendship. Reciprocation is expected.
- Never say, "Let's go Dutch,"[46] or "Let's split the bill."

FORMAL HOSPITALITY

People from Formal cultures expect full hospitality. Hospitality takes on a different definition than it does for Americans. They do not really understand "Make yourself at home," or "Help yourself to what's in the fridge." They expect you to serve them the food, and they expect that as the guest you will offer them the best portion. Potluck is an American concept that is confusing for other cultures, but is readily appreciated because it includes the larger group. Although, if, as an American, you offer to bring a salad or dessert to the house of someone from a Formal culture who invited you to dinner (an offer much appreciated in the USA), they may feel insulted that you might think they can't supply enough food. Liquor, flowers, or chocolates usually suffice.

Hospitality for Formal cultures entails you as the Host/Hostess picking them up at the airport, driving them around town, paying for restaurants, and taking them back to the airport – all at your expense. And, they may ask to stay for 2-4 weeks.

When attempting to be a proper host/hostess, remember the Rule of 3. The **Rule of 3** is to offer your guest something at least three times before you accept that they really do mean "no." (Of course, they could be saying "yes" just to save face!). This can happen with the bill at a restaurant or an attempt to offer the spare room to another family member, for example. Here's another example:

Host: Please try this delicacy.

Guest: No, I couldn't. Thank you.

---

[46] Note in some places "Dutch" is replaced with "American."

Host: I insist.

Guest: I am so full.

Host: Really. I can't let you leave without you trying one.

Guest: (accepting delicacy)...Okay, thank you very much. (Or, not accepting delicacy... "You are much too hospitable. I must return another time soon to appreciate your hospitality.")

The Rule of 3 is also used to affirm understanding in a verbal contract. When I hopped into a taxi with my American colleague in Beijing, I showed the driver the address of our meeting location. He responded by showing me a laminated sheet that indicated the price of the fare in English. The Mandarin way of saying "yes" or "ok" (*hao*) has the intonation of a question; so, it sounds like "How?" I told the taxi driver, "Hao." He pointed to the sheet again, and I responded, "Hao." He tapped it a third time as I said, "Hao," at which point my colleague responded, "I don't KNOW how!"

CHAPTER 19

CONTROL OVER ENVIRONMENT/ FATE (DESTINY)

"Qué será, será. Whatever will be, will be. The future's not ours you see." - song written in 1956 by Jay Livingston and Ray Evans

Control over Environment is the preference to change the environment to fit human needs. This is demonstrated by employees "going the extra mile" – outside of their expected role responsibilities to meet, perhaps unrealistic, expectations. It is the train tunnel being carved straight through the mountain, as opposed to designed to go around it. A common perception by Fate cultures of Control over Environment cultures is that the latter are sometimes insufferable or rash.

The customary cultural value preference of the United States is the tendency to exert control over situations. On one occasion, I was taking a flight from San Francisco on Southwest Airlines in the early evening of Halloween. The passengers were all boarded and the flight attendant informed us there was a maintenance delay. Within 10-15 minutes, four people angrily protested with the flight attendant about the delay, yelling about having parties to attend and so forth. One person actually stormed off the aircraft. Southwest has the safest record in the airline industry, yet these particular people were virulently contentious; not just upset. A woman from Bosnia-Herzegovina said to me, "In my country, we wake up every morning expecting things to *not* work out as desired, and we're glad when they do. Americans expect everything to work out as they desire, and complain a *lot* when it doesn't."

Fate is the preference of the environment to shape how each day, week, or season is played out. External forces, such as weather, God, or unforeseeable events (e.g. "bird flu") may directly change the course of the business environment. A common perception by Control over Environment cultures of Fate cultures is that they are sometimes not proactive, do not take initiative, or are overly complacent.

CHAPTER 20

INSTRUMENTAL/EXPRESSIVE

"Snap out of it!" – Cher as Loretta Castorini in Moonstruck, 1987

Instrumental is the preference of maintaining control of emotion in all gestures and voice. Emotion is selectively[47] displayed to add emphasis to sincerity of a message. A common perception by Expressive cultures of Instrumental cultures is that they are stoic, cold, and/or robotic.

Expressive is the preference of releasing emotion in gestures and voice. All emotions are considered healthy. These cultures, for example, make a lot more noise while grieving at funerals (e.g. Ethiopians). I once had an Italian client who said he felt he could follow the nature of a conversation more or less by merely observing from across the street two Italians engaging in discourse. A common perception by Instrumental cultures of Expressive cultures is that they are dramatic and have a tendency to exaggerate.

---

[47] Dr. Paul Ekman has proven that microexpressions register across a person's face and voice. Microexpressions are uncontrollable, authentic gestures of our emotions that we subconsciously express.

CHAPTER 21

CHANGE/TRADITION

"They paved paradise and put up a parking lot."
– Joni Mitchell, Big Yellow Taxi

Change is the preference to replace the old with something new. New is better; old is devalued. The wheel must be re-invented. Paradise is removed and a parking lot is in its place because it is needed for the airport, for example. Another example is how the Napa Valley regulates the size of its street signs, so as to not appear too touristy and to retain its natural and pristine look. A common perception by Tradition cultures of Change cultures is that they are too hasty and make waste of what is still "good."

    Tradition is the preference to maintain whatever processes are in place because they work and/or are comfortable. There is no need to re-invent the wheel if quality has been attained. People from the cultures of Tradition tend to play up the "Glory Days" of when their culture(s) were at its zenith. A common perception by Change cultures of Tradition cultures is that they are stubborn and old-fashioned.

CHAPTER 22

FIXED TIME/ FLUID TIME

Fixed Time is the preference to keep a schedule punctual. There is often as associated feeling or anxiety that there is not enough time to finish the objective. A common perception by Fluid Time cultures of Fixed Time cultures is that they stress too much and need to loosen up.

Italian to USA:

"I always remember that the funniest thing you told me was about the etiquette for social dinners in the US and the rule of 3 hours. Well, it turned out to be true, even though now with some of my friends they hang out longer at times. Anyhow, it is just a funny thing I always remember and at times mention to my friends when I tell them about my orientation training on US etiquette."

Fluid Time is the preference to keep a schedule that allows the individual to enjoy the moment. The feeling is often that there is plenty of time to finish the objective, even if the deadline is minutes away. The common perception by Fixed Time cultures of Fluid Time cultures is that they have a "mañana" mentality and are procrastinators.

Frantic Voicemail

Wayne: Pablo, this is Wayne. We have just seen on the news that there are wild fires that look to be surrounding your neighborhood. Cars are covered in ash. People and animals are being evacuated. It looks horrendous. We are very concerned about your welfare and that of your family's. Please contact us immediately so we can rest assured that you are alright.

Question: Should Pablo call his boss Wayne? Pablo just got in to Portland from Oakland and Wayne is on the east coast. The time is 9:13 p.m. PST.

Addendum:

Pablo decided to not call Wayne until the next morning, which he made a concerted effort to do at 6 a.m. PST (West Coast)/9 a.m. EST (East Coast). When he reached Wayne and explained that he didn't want to wake Wayne up with the news of his safety, Wayne responded that he was glad Pablo decided not to wake him up. This left Pablo with a feeling that Americans are superficial. He wondered, Why did Wayne express so much concern about Pablo's safety from the "horrendous fires" if those concerns are only valid during waking hours?

<u>French to USA</u>: ·

"It's funny how so many Americans try to find the closest parking spot to the restaurant. We, French, just park anywhere and are fine to walk the extra distance."

CHAPTER 23

EQUALITY (EGALITARIAN)/ HIERARCHY (POWER DISTANCE)

Equality is the preference of treating others at *your* level, despite differences in gender, race, religion, age, weight, title, education, sexual orientation, marital status, number of children, dress, or socio-economic status. These cultures tend to be Protestant. The boss is often seen as a resourceful democrat. The common perception by Hierarchical cultures of Equality cultures is that they lack social protocol and can, therefore, be embarrassing.

<u>American to Middle East</u>:

"For me the key to success is to go places and do things where you feel mainstreamed. After a short time---you quickly find the times and places to go where you feel comfortable. Either by experience or word of mouth you can easily define the parameters of your comfort zone.

Social injustice is still my BIGGEST problem. My houseboy is not allowed to have his mother visit because he has a lowly job and is from a looked-down-upon country. After he tried to get a visa for her, I took a day off to go with him and tried to see if I could get a visa for her---the "officials" just laughed and spit on the ground...and told me not to waste my time. He is an employee of a large company (we have tried to sponsor him, but the company will not release him). We pay (about $400 USD). The company in turn pays him (about $105 USD). He has been here 10 years and has never gotten a pay raise and recently, because of increases cost of living, his salary was reduced. Needless to say, this is an easy one for me to fix...give him more money, buy him food and clothing, let him use our car so he can go to church...but he is only one of thousands.

Julian says to just look at Los Angeles and there is social injustice all over the place. I agree...but in the US you have a chance (if you take it) to be more---to rise above--to be educated--that doesn't exist here.

I've been AMERICAN too long and still naïvely believe in the American dream."

Hierarchy is the preference of treating others at *their* level according to differences in gender, race, religion, age, weight, title, education, sexual orientation, marital status, number of children, dress, or socio-economic status. It is marginalization. These cultures typically have one, two, or all three of what I call the **"Triumvirate of Hierarchy"**:

1. **Military History** (Dictatorship- General down to soldier)
2. **Catholicism** (Papacy- Pope down to sinner)
3. **Monarchy** (Royals- King down to peasant)

People in these cultures "know their rank" and find it difficult or impossible to talk back, disagree with a superior's idea, or "jump over someone's head." A common American oversight is to promote someone from a Hierarchical culture who is a great "soldier" (meritocracy), who then turns into a monster of a boss. Such was the case with one French executive at a US-based company, who attested that "good" bosses must behave with superior, authoritarian actions. The Hierarchical boss is often seen as the benevolent autocrat or paternalistic figure. A common perception by Equality cultures of Hierarchical cultures is that they need to be "knocked off their high horse" (American) or to "cut down the tall poppy" (Australian).

Be aware that Hierarchical cultures are not the type to appreciate "rags to riches" stories. These stories about entrepreneurs and/or "self-made" people are not understood by the status cultures, leaving them bewildered as to why you would wish to speak of such humble origins. For example, elderly Argentines still gather around Eva Perón's grave to argue and dispute her reputation as a "whore," since she was from the working class ("the wrong side of the tracks") and was only lucky enough to become First Lady by first acting as a mistress. People from Hierarchical cultures like to throw out superfluous pieces of information, such as who in their family is a doctor.

CHAPTER 24

PRIVATE SPACE/ PUBLIC SPACE

Private Space is the preference of keeping an amplified personal bubble. Americans consider this amplification to be a full-arm's length. If someone enters the Private Space there must be one of four reasons in order for it to be okay: 1) s/he is invited into that intimate space (e.g. family member, lover, etc.), 2) something needs to be whispered, 3) it was an accident, 4) public transportation is crowded (which is what makes elevators uncomfortable for many Americans). Note that much of this behavior is determined by greeting. Kissing cultures don't kiss and run back; so they tend to have Public Space. Conversely, bowing cultures[48] don't bow and run forward; so they tend to have an even greater need for Private Space. A common perception by Public Space cultures of Private Space cultures is that they are skittish or odd.

<u>American to England:</u>

"No one talks on the tube...the 'in' thing to do is read the free Metro paper on the tube. There's also very little eye contact but it doesn't bother me."

Interestingly, Americans seem to contradict their preference for Private Space when it comes to their homes. This is because the American Dream is to own your own home...to be the King/Queen of your castle. Consequently, visitors are sometimes invited, or ask, to take a tour or a "look around the place." Closets, bedrooms, and

---

[48] There are always exceptions. The train in Japan is one.

bathrooms are viewed. No other culture in the world practices this behavior.

Public Space is the preference for "intimate" proximity, meaning close-range. These cultures appear to Americans to have no boundaries. Arabs not only get close, they may even hold hands. Latinos may rest a hand on your shoulder. American men tend to be "homophobic" and prefer to not be touched by other men or to have their Private Space "invaded." Notice how many American men love to spread their knees wide open while they sit, which then results in them allowing a bar stool or movie theater seat to remain open between them, if possible. The common perception by Private Space cultures of Public Space cultures is that they are "coming on" to them.

I have often had people ask me how many kisses one should greet another when meeting someone from a kissing culture. Paris usually offers just 2, but some places practice 5. For a "kissing map," please follow this link: http://combiendebises.free.fr. There is a legend beneath the map of France to act as a guideline.

Latin America, in general, greets with one kiss, but Italy, Spain, and France mostly do just two. When greeting someone with a kiss where this is customary, there are some important rules to remember.

- It's okay to touch the person you are about to kiss greet. Maybe you'd like to hold them by the upper arms.

- Always start kissing in the direction you would shake the person's hand, which is typically *your left*.

- Unless you are a relative, a godfather, or maybe you're in Turkey, men only kiss women; not other men. Women kiss men and women.

- You can 1) air kiss, 2) press cheeks and make the kissing sound, 3) actually place your lips on the person's cheeks (just partial, not the whole mouth press on both sides – which is hard to do, if you're both attempting the same thing simultaneously).

Puerto Rican to Turkey:

"In Puerto Rico we kiss the women; so we were already half-way there. It was not a big deal for me to kiss the men."

CHAPTER 25

COMPETITION/ COOPERATION

Competition is the preference of outperforming someone else in order to improve one's standing. In the USA, we find this to be healthy. Healthy competition is seen as a form of motivation to improve oneself. Unhealthy competition is considered ruthless. This is when, for example, UC Irvine Medical students vying for the top grades, tear out required reading pages from reference books in the library; or, when someone at work takes credit for your efforts because you didn't speak up to claim it for yourself. In these examples, there is no true competition...it is the attempt for others to get ahead, and they are not truly *outperforming*. As such, a common perception by Cooperative cultures of Competitive cultures is that they are backstabbing and intense.

The Olympics is clearly a world competition. For the Winter 2010 Olympics games, we can see that the USA was in the lead with the count of medals, and tying with Germany in number of Gold medals, for three of four medal events. [49]

---

49 Monday, February 22, 2010. Data from the "Medals Table" from USA Today, February 24, 2010.

Nation	Gold	Silver	Bronze	Total
USA	7	7	10	**24**
Germany	7	9	5	21
Norway	6	3	5	14
Russia	2	3	5	10
Canada	4	4	1	9
South Korea	4	4	1	9
Austria	3	3	3	9
France	2	2	4	8
Switzerland	5	0	2	7
Sweden	3	2	2	7

Here is the power of statistics. If we were to take into consideration the population of each country, then Norway is clearly the fiercest competitor of the bunch in Gold medals and in overall medals coming in at 906. Its population is 64.7 times smaller than the population of the USA. And, at the time of this publication, they're already coming in third place! It is fair to make a qualitative conclusion that Norwegians, on average, are much more fit than the average American, and that the odds of you encountering an Olympian in Oslo are fairly high. The medals would look more like the following graph:

Nation	Gold	Silver	Bronze	Total
USA (304m)	7	7	10	24
Germany (82m)	7→26	9→33	5→19	21→78
Norway (4.7m)	**6→388**	3→194	5→324	14→**906**
Russia (142m)	2→4	3→6	5→10	10→20
Canada (33m)	4→36	4→36	1→9	9→81
S. Korea (49m)	4→24	4→24	1→6	9→54
Austria (8m)	3→114	3→114	3→114	9→342
France (62m)	2→10	2→10	4→20	8→40
Switzerland (7.6m)	5→200	0→0	2→80	7→280
Sweden (9m)	3→102	2→68	2→68	7→238

Cooperation is the preference of equalizing performance so that it is extended to all within the group. Credit is to be shared. One Brazilian could not understand why her boss kept insisting that she would be sure to pass along to the Executive Director that the Brazilian was the one who came up with the great Marketing idea...she kept telling her boss that she would like to share the credit with the Marketing team. A common perception by Competitive cultures of Cooperative cultures is that they are very giving and lack ambition.

CHAPTER 26

PRESENT-FUTURE/ PAST ORIENTATION

"There's no time like the present." – American saying

Present-Future Orientation[50] is the preference of only considering what is pertinent in the moment and the immediate future. This future can extend up to a year, or 3-5, but usually not beyond. In the USA, we are interested in "the here & the now." Overall, we endeavor to learn from our mistakes, and we choose not to dwell. There is rarely a projection of 25-50 years, like in China. The USA has a history of roughly 200 years, which is not much, relatively speaking, when compared to countries which have been around for millennia. We consider a house constructed in the 1920's as old; whereas, a European may consider a building constructed in the 1490's as new.

Men tend to be more Present-oriented. They have been known to make comments such as, "Anything we said 6 months ago is inadmissible in an argument. In fact, all comments become null and void after 7 days." A common perception by Past-oriented cultures of Present-Future-oriented cultures is that they do not see the big picture (tunnel vision) and are hasty.

Past Orientation is the preference of only considering the historical highpoints of its culture/experience. Many former empires hold fast to their traditions because once upon a time they "ruled the

---

[50] This time orientation can be broken down into 3 groups, but I've taken the liberty to just make it 2.

world." E.g. France, England, China, Greece, Italy, Egypt, Iraq (Mesapotamia).

Germans, among other cultures which have survived harrowing times such as the rationing during the World Wars, have often asked me why Americans spend money they don't have on credit cards, instead of waiting to make the desired purchase with money they *do* have on a debit card. The answer is that Americans are Present-oriented; they want it NOW.

Women tend to be more Past-oriented. They have been known to make comments such as, "I won't go to that conference, if [nemesis from umpteen years ago] is going to be there." A common perception by Present-Future-oriented cultures of Past-oriented cultures is that they need to stop looking over their shoulder so much and live in the now.

CHAPTER 27

PRACTICAL (PRAGMATIC/EFFICIENCY)/ IDEALISM

"I don't care if it's a white cat or a black cat. It's a good cat so long as it catches mice." – Deng Xiaoping

Practical is the focus on maximizing the objective at the lowest financial cost, time-associated cost, and risk. For example, consider the American businesswoman who boards the trolley in San Francisco in her nice dress suit and tennis shoes. An idealist (e.g. a French businesswoman) would find that ensemble revolting.

Practical people may give you gifts that they feel you *need*; not necessarily what you *want*. The common perception by Idealists of Practical cultures is that they can be budget-minded and tasteless.

Idealism is the focus on maximizing the objective at a cost to preserve the dream or the aesthetic appeal. The French, for example, can be slaves to fashion. The look is more important than practicality. A common perception by Practical cultures of Idealists is that they can be ridiculous and quixotic.

CHAPTER 28

MATERIALISM/SPIRITUALISM

"Diamonds are a girl's best friend." – Marilyn Monroe[51]

Materialism is the preference of acquiring possessions and placing more value on material objects than personal fulfillment attained intrinsically, without objects. Americans are constantly called Materialists and Capitalists. These adjectives come from the perception that Americans are workaholics.[52] Only the Japanese are known worldwide to match the USA, as a whole. A common perception by Spiritualists of Materialists is that they are misguided.

Spiritualism is the preference of finding intrinsic happiness. Usually, Spiritualists find peace in nature. They don't necessarily require a lot of possessions. A common perception by Materialists of Spiritualists is that they lack ambition and usually follow some philosophy or religion that comes across as "cultish."

Here is a tale which illustrates Materialism/Spiritualism:

An American goes to a small, pristine fishing village on the Mexican Riviera. He encounters a Mexican with a fishing net so full of fish, it looks as though it's about to burst. The American observes the Mexican fisherman is not *selling* the fish, but, rather, *giving* them

---

[51] Line is made famous by Marilyn (1953), but originally sung by Carol Channing (1949) and written by Jule Styne and Leo Robin.

[52] The Japanese (men primarily, as it is a male-dominated workforce) are known for working extremely long hours.

away to the locals! The American approaches the Mexican with his proposition...

American: Hey, if you partner with me, together we could open an office in Mexico City and distribute fish throughout all of Mexico!

Mexican: Ok. And then what?

American: And then, we'll set up an office in Miami and distribute fish throughout all of Latin America!

Mexican: Ok. And then what?

American: And then we'll set up an office in New York City and distribute fish throughout the world!

Mexican: Ok. And then what?

American: Well, then, you can retire early! You can walk here along the beach holding your wife's hand, and watch the sun set!

Mexican: But I'm already doing that!

This tale illustrates the "rat race" that so many Americans face. It is *never* enough. There is a need, thirst, or yearning for more. The contrarians may offer, "There is no luggage rack on a hearse," or, "You can't take it with you when you go."

CHAPTER 29

DOING/BEING

"Just do it." – Nike slogan

Doing is the preference of keeping busy during "down" time. When there is no work present in front of you, people from the Doing cultures find things to do. They are the DIY'ers (Do-It-Yourself'ers) who flock to Home Depot, Lowe's, and other hardware stores to find the materials they need to do more. They pile projects on top of projects and volunteer for tasks which few others want. A common perception by Being cultures of Doing cultures is that they are workaholics and diehard busy bees.

Being is the preference of finding time to unwind. People from this culture may enjoy lying in a hammock, curling up with a good book, hanging out on the porch with friends, etc. They take time to smell the roses, and sip the lemonade. A common perception by Doing cultures of Being cultures is that they lack initiative and responsibility.

CHAPTER 30

MONOCHRONIC/ POLYCHRONIC

Monochronic is the preference of doing one thing at a time. This may be in speech or action. People from this culture strongly believe that one thing must be done at a time in order for it to be done well. It is about quality. They are the ones likely to say, "Please say whatever you have to say during commercials." A common perception by Polychronic cultures of Monochronic cultures is that they are boring and tedious.

    Polychronic is the preference of doing many things at the same time, or multi-tasking. This may be in speech or action. As a result, there is a lot of interrupting and starting/stopping processes. People from this culture strongly believe that many things must be performed concurrently to get the maximum result(s) accomplished. They feel they are maximizers. It is about quantity. A common perception by Monochronic cultures of Polychronic cultures is that they are rude and lack structure.

CHAPTER 31

UNIVERSALISM/ PARTICULARISM

Universalism is applying one rule to all. No one is above the law...as in the case with President Bill Clinton when he was impeached for lying about his relationship with Monica Lewinsky. People with this cultural preference tend to be Protestant. A common perception by Particularists of Universalists is that they lack empathetic understanding and are strict.

For example, generally speaking, Americans take the rules of the road very seriously. People who come from Particularistic cultures (e.g. Latin America) find it "very easy" to drive in the USA, because they find that American drivers follow the rules. They remark how amazing it is that when the street light is red, people stop.

An Australian couple observed that American drivers in California sometimes slow down at stop signs, but don't necessarily come to a full stop and proceed through the intersection. This is called a "California Roll" – which is a play on the name used for the Japanese imitation crab sushi roll here. The Australians, feeling oh-so-cultural, decided to mimic the behavior and were consequently pulled over by the police. They explained to the officer that they witnessed other people do it. Yes, we do it...when the police are NOT around! This is one way how we change the rules: if you won't get caught, and it's safe, many drivers will perform the California Roll.

Particularism is making personal exceptions for a specific few. People with this cultural preference understand *why* the rules exist;

however, they strongly believe that special circumstances and conditions must be taken into consideration. Particularists tend to be Catholic. A common perception by Universalists of Particularists is that they are overly subjective and rule-breakers.

Fons Trompenaars created a values test that he administered to IBM employees worldwide. From the scenarios he created, he plotted the data along the spectrums of each pair of values. For Universalism/Particularism, one scenario that he created is as follows:

Imagine that you are in a car being driven by a good friend. Your friend is exceeding the speed limit by 15 mph. Suddenly, your friend hits a pedestrian. Now his/her lawyer is saying to you that if you testify that your friend was driving the speed limit, s/he could be spared from some serious consequences. What do you do?

Remember, there is no right or wrong answer here. People respond according to how we were taught or by what we learned. Each person is trying to do "right" by the situation. Of course, what is left out of the scenario is the level of subjectivity due to the relationship between the individuals, and the degree of trust we have in our judicial system and/or government. South Korea emerged as the leading Particularist culture surveyed.[53] Roughly 74% of South Koreans would support their friend by saying whatever was needed to relieve him/her of the "serious consequences." Canada surveyed as the most Universalistic, coming in with roughly 96% of the people choosing to testify what they observed to occur on the day of the accident. The USA surveyed a close second with 95% Universalistic. However, if we were to replace the "good friend" with "your mother," the Universalist answers change dramatically to reflect more Particularism, in an effort to "save Mom."[54]

---

[53] Venezuela came in second at 66% Particularistic.

[54] Helpful clients have offered that if "good friend" was replaced with "your mother-in-law," the answers would unequivocally reflect Canadian Universalism.

Particularists find a "loophole" in the law that "allows" certain behaviors. Consider the following article which comes from a culture (Qatar) that only permits sex within marriage:

"Wife for vacation: Qataris marry poor women just for the holidays![55]

DOHA • A novel trend is emerging in the Qatari society whereby mostly already married men apparently bored with their existing wives, pick a new spouse to spend time with during holidaying abroad in the summer months, reports a local Arabic daily.

Young women who are from poor families, divorcees and widows are the ones who are mostly available for such temporary marriages. 'The phenomenon is widespread in other GCC states, but gradually it is spreading to Qatar as well. There have been a few instances of such marriages taking place here,' the daily quoted a Qatari woman social worker as saying.

The man who picks such a wife, divorces her after his summer vacation overseas has ended. 'The women who are going in for such marriages look only for fun and financial benefits,' said the social worker.

Such temporary weddings are leaving an adverse impact on society and need to be checked, she added. According to the social worker, the mushrooming of TV channels and information explosion is to blame for the unprecedented trend.

The end-sufferer in this nasty game, which will lead to more divorces, are (sic) the wife and children of the man who is

---

[55] Source: THE PENINSULA, Web posted at: 8/6/2006.

going in for temporary marriage. 'I suggest that instead of going in for a temporary marriage, one should have a full-fledged second marriage. This way, the second wife will have her rights protected,' said the social worker.

Higher costs of conventional marriage and added responsibilities are the main causes of why men prefer to have a temporary wife during summer holidaying abroad.

As for younger and unmarried people going in for such temporary marriages, there is a need to provide them financial assistance so that they can opt for traditional marriage, said the social worker."

American to Switzerland:

"Luzern is filled with hidden cameras for speeding and the speed limits are absurdly low (30 km/h[56] in many streets!). My first week of driving was a disaster. I was disoriented because I didn't know the road signs (my company really should provide some assistance with this) and I drove 50 km[57] in a 30 km zone 3 times in one week.

About a month later, I got a letter telling me they were taking my license away! And I paid more than 3000 CHF ($2,900 USD) in fines. It was only for one month that I lost the license, but it was a rather unpleasant bit of culture shock! *The locals know exactly where the cameras are, so they speed everywhere, except just as they pass by the trap.*[58] After this happened to me, I found out that the same thing has happened to many new people at <company>."

---

[56] 30 km/h is less than 19 mph. 1 kilometer = .621 mile

[57] 50 km/h is roughly 31 mph.

[58] Emphasis added to show connection to cultural preference of Particularism.

CHAPTER 32

TOLERANCE FOR AMBIGUITY (RISK-TAKERS)/ NEED FOR CERTAINTY (RISK-AVERSE)

Tolerance for Ambiguity (Risk-Takers) is the preference to continue or move forward with a decision despite not having all of the information. Americans are known for being extreme Risk-Takers. A common perception by Need for Certainty cultures of Tolerance for Ambiguity cultures is that they are rash and impulsive.

Need for Certainty (Risk-Averse) is the preference to not move forward with any decisions until all of the information has been discussed. As a result, things can take a *long* time. For example, several more meetings must be held, all functional specifications must be read before proceeding to test any software, etc. A common perception by Tolerance for Ambiguity cultures of Need for Certainty cultures is that they are overly meticulous, cumbersome, and stubborn.

CHAPTER 33

THE ROI OF REPATRIATION

<u>Swiss Romand to Brazil:</u>

"I can tell you, the longer you stay outside of your home country, the more difficult it is to come back...because you change and your country does in a different way."

Foreign assignments have become increasingly important as companies strive to tap into resources around the globe. Multinationals and transnational organizations send their expatriates, typically from 18 months to 3 years, to live overseas as a way to transfer the knowledge and culture from headquarters. These "expatriates" typically have influential positions, either from title or from merely coming from headquarters. Many companies, such as Johnson & Johnson, send only those they assess to be in the top performance category (i.e. Hi-Po's, or high potentials) to take on a foreign assignment.

An alarming percentage of attrition exists among those repatriates who have successfully completed their assignments overseas. **One study estimates that 26% of repatriates leave the company within two years of their return,[59] while another reports that up to 75% consider leaving their employers either during or after working abroad.[60]**

---

[59] Windham International, 1999

[60] Pricewaterhouse Coopers & Cranfield University, 2007

<u>American Repatriating from Switzerland:</u>

"I cannot say we are doing as well as we had hoped. It has been very difficult for me to transition back to work and Jeffrey is having a hard time deciding whether he should work or not. He is only half-heartedly approaching looking for a job, and although I know he does not want to work again, he is not sure what to do with his life. It makes things very stressful right now. But we will continue to work through it. If I remember your class, this is about the time when we will be at our lowest with respect to repatriation, so we just need to hang in there for now. Unfortunately my work takes me traveling too much, so a trip for the family to get away is not in the plans!"

<u>Belgian Repatriating from USA:</u>

"Coming back and reintegrating back in Belgium seems to be more difficult than going to the States."

I conducted an action research study on "high potentials" from 26 Fortune 500 companies to uncover **the relationship between cultural adaptability and successful re-entry**. My finding was that **organizations are most likely to lose those expatriates who are sent to cultures which have values vastly different from American values.** On average, 33% of those surveyed decided to leave the company which sent them overseas within two years of their return.

Losing and replacing a middle manager can cost an organization up to 100% of his/her salary.[61] The average expatriate assignment cost per annum is $311,000.[62] Tie this together with the reality that there are 76 million Baby Boomers and only 44 million Gen X'ers. These statistics indicate that any organization using an expatriate program

---

[61] Prudential Resources Management, 1997

[62] Pricewaterhouse Coopers & Cranfield University, 2007

must determine its efficiency as part of its talent management strategy, in order to compete effectively in the "War for Talent."

Bear in mind that many repatriates expect that the return back to their "home country" is simpler than the relocation to the "host country." Lack of preparation on behalf of the repatriate, as well as the company, coupled with the complexity of the family stress create a high risk for attrition. They experience more physical symptoms and external emotional pressures than expected, which result in more re-entry, or reverse, cultural shock. Also, the symptoms of reverse culture shock manifest more quickly than within the outbound move. The stress symptoms generally appear in a variety of ways: physically, behaviorally, and emotionally. (See chapter on Cultural Shock).

A review of the literature revealed four categories of emotional competencies necessary for employees to be successful leaders:

1. Self-Awareness
2. Social Awareness
3. Self-Management
4. Relationship Management

ACTION RESEARCH STUDY

While I interviewed over 70 executives, only 31 executives fit the profile parameters for the study. These high potentials accepted assignments which ranged from 18 months to 3 years. Together they represented a total of 26 companies. The gender breakdown was 74% male and 26% female. Ages ranged from 30-49.

The metrics, or "value dials," in the instrument used in the research measured the changes before the assignment and post-assignment. The value dials determine whether significant value shifts away from the United States culture have caused a reason for talent to be difficult to retain. Of course, one limitation to this instrument is the self-report bias may underscore modesty or exaggerate claims of improvement.

MASCULINITY-FEMINITY STUDY

Previous research has indicated that emotional intelligence (EQ) usually increases and the values shift when employees are subjected to different environmental contexts. This is known as part of what is called **Social Cognitive Theory** - how people think and under what type of milieu they operate.

The research data that I collected in my study suggests that **those repatriates who relocated into overseas cultures farther away from their own American cultural values, that is, into "feminine cultures," experience the highest numbers of employee attrition.** The United States is defined as a "masculine culture."

Dutch cultural anthropologist Geert Hofstede "genderfied" cultures as masculine or feminine. He defined masculinity as follows: "Masculinity pertains to societies in which social gender roles are clearly distinct -- that is, men are supposed to be assertive, tough, and focused on material success, whereas women are supposed to be more modest, tender, and concerned with the quality of life. Femininity pertains to societies in which social gender roles overlap -- that is, both men and women are supposed to be modest, tender, and concerned with the quality of life."[63]

Masculine cultures are most attracted to the following:
a) High earnings

b) Recognition for a job well done

c) Advancement

---

[63] Hofstede, p. 82

d) Challenging work, from which the individual (value of Individualism) can get a sense of accomplishment

Masculine manages are lone decision-makers who search for facts and data, rather than lead a group discussion.

Feminine cultures are most attracted to the following:

a) Having a good relationship with the manager/supervisor
b) Cooperative work environment
c) Desirable living area
d) Employment security

Feminine managers are less visible, intuitive rather than decisive, and generally seek out consensus.

In my study, American repatriates returning from feminine host countries, found themselves (i.e. Self-Awareness) to have developed **higher diplomatic skills in communication, are more open-minded to variances of opinion, and are more inclusive of others whose styles vary from their own**. These attributes tend to be associated with the feminine values of Cooperation and Relationship as opposed to the masculine values of Competition and Task.

Success in adapting to a host culture creates flexibility. This flexibility is denoted in the increased emotional and cultural intelligence that expatriates gather with experience (i.e. Social Awareness) which, in turn, leads them to become better leaders. Expatriates act accordingly in their own home cultures (i.e. Self-Management) and consciously determine which other behaviors are most effective in the host culture (i.e. Relationship Management). These new behaviors repeated over time become natural. When the host culture is strongly more feminine, then there is a higher likelihood of a cultural mismatch of the repatriate with his/her organization upon return to the United States, as suggested in the survey results.

FINDINGS

The findings showed that companies are most likely to lose those expatriates who are sent to cultures which have values vastly different from American values – rendering repatriation programs as critical upon their return. The role played by cultural variance of host and home cultures is that the greater the cultural variance of the host culture from the home culture, the more likely it is for companies to lose the investment placed in those employees.

The study indicated that 50% of those in the "most different values" cultural block chose to leave their organization, versus 36% of those within the *same* cultural block. Interesting to note, however, those who chose to leave the company experienced, on average, *less* re-entry shock symptoms than those who chose to stay. This suggests that **it is not necessarily the frequency of the symptoms, but the severity, gravity, or depth of the symptoms** that creates so much dissatisfaction and generates the readiness of the repatriate to change his/her circumstances.

Table 1- Masculine/Feminine and Individualist/Collectivistic Dimensions

Individualist Masculine	Individualist Feminine	Collectivistic Masculine	Collectivistic Feminine
Australia	Denmark	Arabic Countries	Brazil
Austria	Finland	Argentina	Costa Rica
Belgium	France	Colombia	Chile
Canada	Israel	Ecuador	Dominican Republic*
Germany	Netherlands	Greece	El Salvador
Great Britain	Norway	Hong Kong	Guatemala

Ireland	Puerto Rico**	India	Indonesia
South Africa	Spain	Jamaica	Iran
Switzerland	Sweden	Japan	Korea
United States		Malaysia	Panama
		Mexico	Peru
		Pakistan	Portugal
		Philippines	Singapore*
		Venezuela	Taiwan
			Thailand
			Turkey

* Indicates that these cultures are added to Hofstede's list by the researcher (i.e. R. Gil).

** Indicates that Puerto Rico is acknowledged as a commonwealth of the USA, however it retains much of its 500-year Spanish cultural heritage to be worthy of being mentioned separately.

THEMES

Five themes emerged from the results of this study:

1. **Shift of Values** – most notably from Competition to Cooperation

2. **Nostalgia** – 53% of those surveyed experienced an overwhelming nostalgia and longing to go back to the same country to which they had expatriated

3. **Global Serial Assignment Urges** – to repeat the same rewarding challenges overseas

4. **Displacement** – feelings of being an outsider in their home country offices, e.g. 29% large scale

reorganization; 47% cited perception by others as talking excessively about their foreign experiences

5. **Personal Life Issues** – usually with family.

<u>American to Spain, on to England</u>:

"Sometimes, I think that we've worked so hard and imposed on others for assistance, and now we are just leaving it all behind. That's where the sadness comes in. I feel sorry for all the people who have worked so hard to help us and I feel like we are turning our backs and leaving them empty-handed. In particular, I think of the personal assistant to Caleb's boss, who has been our lifeline since long before we arrived. She's an *enchufe*[64] with a heart of gold, and she works very hard and generously for others. She gets left behind, while Caleb and his boss head off to London. There is no longer an equivalent position for her here, so I don't know what she will do for work and I know that she loved her job. I also think of the teachers at the kids' school, and how much personal interest they took in helping them get started. I know that some of them take great satisfaction in what they have accomplished in my children's development. But I also know that some of them feel it is hard on the kids to uproot them so frequently, and that makes me feel guilty, like I am not making the best choices as a parent. I am having a hard time getting Mason's teacher to fill-out reference forms for the schools in London. I don't know if he is just busy with all the final exams, etc., or if it's a signal that deep-down he thinks we are making a mistake and, therefore, doesn't consider the forms to be a priority. I have spoken to him a few times in the last week, but it's always been rushed.

---

[64] Enchufe means "connector" or "liaison."

The main thing I am writing about, though, is saying (my) goodbyes. I think of all the people along the way who helped us and made us feel welcome and cared-for. From our friends, to the teachers, the moms at the school, and even the woman at the dry cleaner – I cry when I think about saying goodbye to them, and I don't know how to say thank you for things that seem trivial, but really touched us. And I don't want to forget anyone. I agree with you, a pricey gift means much less than something personal."

The acknowledgment and/or desire for personal and family counseling[65] was a recurring theme of 23% of those who participated in the survey. Familial pressures and an overwhelming sense of personal responsibility felt burdensome and consuming, which lessened productivity and ultimately led some to sever themselves from the company entirely. Despite Corporate America's seeming preference to separate private, personal life from work to a certain degree, the distractions posed by these familial pressures cannot be underestimated. Employees will lose productivity in the workplace by unintentionally "zoning out" or by drifting into thoughts about their current pressing concerns.

The fourth and fifth themes of Displacement and Personal Life Issues are the top causes of failure to assimilate well during the *repatriation process in the home country.* (Interesting to note...these are the same two causes of assignment failure for expatriates). It is easy, then, to understand why 53% of those surveyed felt an overwhelming nostalgia and a longing to go back overseas.

---

[65] Employee Assistance Program (EAP) is typically offered by companies, but seldom mentioned. They are funds used for counseling of all types and EAP is extended to family members of the employee.

<u>American to Peru:</u>

"We did have to learn how to cook and clean again, and the youngest needed to learn to live without his nanny and then to speak English (he probably spoke more Spanish upon the move, and his English is still lagging). The rest of the kids seemed quite happy to return to the States and speak English, but honestly miss many of the opportunities that they had in Arequipa (probably mostly the sporting opportunities and other similar extracurricular activities with high level coaching).

I'd go back overseas in a heartbeat. It was a once-in-a-lifetime type of opportunity where we grew tremendously, and I hope to be able to repeat it."

Companies that endure and remain strong in the marketplace are those which illustrate a passion for change. This type of "built to change" culture must permeate all levels of the organization: individual, interpersonal, group, inter-group, and the full organization. Structure, talent systems, and rewards can be reconfigured to support an openness to change. Those organizations which breed a comfort level with change can, by virtue of their culture, assist with the return of their executives from overseas assignments.

As defined by one human resource executive, "Maximizing our Return on Investment (ROI) is not simply successfully completing the assignment, but bringing back the increased company knowledge and history to the home company so that we may benefit." Those who stay with the company are considered to have returned the value on the investment made; those who do not, create a loss on ROI for the company.

Upon re-entry, the repatriate does not return as the same person. This is an opportunity for Human Resources to interview the "new" candidate when s/he returns. Career Management and the development of innovative Corporate Strategies are critical at this stage. It would be best to involve many stakeholders after a human resources assessment is conducted.

And, given that the national demographic percentages of Latinos and Asians are increasing at a rapid pace, the United States is shifting towards the more feminine cultural values. There may lay some new opportunities within the home market for these repatriates.

CHAPTER 34

IN A NUTSHELL (SUMMARY)

"It is the past that gives us our identity and corrals our behavior in order to preserve that identity." – Peter Block

Many people like to tell themselves and others that we all want the same thing. They may even point to Abraham Maslow's pyramid, the Hierarchy of Needs and say we all need the same things. The truth is, all of us have needs, but not all of us have all the same needs (or ever reach what Maslow refers to as Self-Actualization.

"Homeostasis" is at the base of the pyramid. **Homeostasis** is an internal, stable condition of a living organism. French physiologist Claude Bernard referred to the same concept as *milieu interieur* (internal environment). The system, or organism, survives because there are multiple, constantly-changing, balancing adjustments and reactions occurring to keep everything feeling secure. With this in mind, **the answer(s) to survival, culture, and life are literally within us: we must adapt**. This does not mean that one needs to change the identifiable core beliefs and values that one has; *au contraire*, "maintaining a constancy of identifiable core beliefs and values is the key to true stability throughout life."[66] Straying from your core values often leads to discontent.[67]

---

[66] Pollock & Van Reken, <u>Third Culture Kids</u>, pg. 177.

[67] Indeed, what you valued in your high school years is usually the point of regression later in life.

Keep these following tips in mind to be successful in understanding how to "read your opponent's playbook":

- Be aware of your own culture in terms of values, beliefs, and behaviors. This includes your cultural filters and stereotypes.

- Know what triggers you. Work on diminishing them so that you don't give your power away.

- Allow room for multiple interpretations of a situation, rather than sticking to your first interpretation.

- Practice Inquiry and Active Listening.

- Describe, Interpret, and share Expectations.

- Develop empathy. Try to see the situation from another's perspective.

- Don't assume the other person thinks just like you.

If you don't remember these tips, don't sweat it. Like the old adage goes, practice makes perfect. You are bound to do well professionally and personally if you value relationships, have curiosity, have a tolerance for uncertainty, are flexible, empathetic, have a strong sense of self, have a sense of humor (at yourself and of situations), and can demonstrate patience and respect. Without these traits, an executive would not be a strong candidate for an overseas assignment.

One fictional account of a man on a mission towards self-actualization is The Alchemist, by Paulo Coelho. An alchemist is one who practices alchemy, which is the process of developing something of little value into something of great value. The protagonist leaves home only to return home and find that he could not have experienced such wealth and happiness at home if he did not venture out into the world.

It always boils down to respect, adaptation, and the choice to leave. You change, or the other person changes, or you leave. So, if you are not going to tip the waiter/waitress 15-20% in the USA, don't eat at a full-service restaurant. If you are not going to adhere to the rules of the bride, don't go to the wedding. If you are not going to refrain from smoking or cursing in a home which does not practice those behaviors, don't visit those people. You have entered their environment. And, ultimately, if you are not going to be respectful of Rome by following the expected norms of Rome when in Rome, just stay home.

GLOSSARY

Active Listening is listening for implied meaning, not necessarily the literal. The attention is focused on the speaker. Judgment is suspended.

Anger is a secondary emotion to pain.

Appreciative Inquiry is a tool used to focus on what works, rather than trying to fix what doesn't.

Assimilation is when the less dominant group mimics cultural traits or behaviors of the dominant or more influential members of a particular culture.

Auditory learner is one who learns well simply by listening.

Being-orientation is the preference of finding time to unwind without much regard to time.

Boomer is one born on and/or between the years of 1946 – 1964.

Change is situational. It happens when anything begins or ends in our lives, and it is external.

Change-orientation is the preference to replace the old with something new.

Chromatics is communication through colors.

Chronemics is communication through use of time within a culture.

Competition-orientation is the preference of outperforming, or the attempt to one-up, someone else in order to improve one's standing.

Collectivism is the focus on whichever social circles to which you belong (e.g. families, organizations, alumni groups, etc.). These groups support you in exchange for loyalty.

Competing Values Model holds that power resides in the integration approach of the four major culture types: Clan/Family, Hierarchy/Eiffel, Market/Missile, Adhocracy/Incubator.

Continental Dining is keeping the fork in the left hand and the knife in the right hand while one eats – never shall the twain change hands.

Contribution Recognition is the comprehension of what you have contributed to a situation.

Control over Environment-orientation is the preference of the environment being changed to fit human needs.

Cooperation-orientation is the preference of equalizing performance so that it is extended to all within the group.

Covert Revelation is an indirect form of communication practiced when the instigator portrays him/herself as the messenger of another; and/or allows some kind of self-communication.

Cultural Adjustment Curve is the model used to represent the five stages of assimilation to change (i.e. Pre-Departure, Tourist, Degenerative, Culture Shock; Full Acceptance).

Cultural Baggage is the set of values one brings to a new culture and begins to apply them.

Cultural Iceberg is a model used to illustrate Values, Beliefs, and Assumptions as they lead to manifest Behavior that is seen and/or heard.

Cultural Imperialism is when the way you do things becomes extinct because your style has been consumed by another more dominant style.

Cultural Intelligence (Cultural Quotient or **CQ)** is full understanding of your own culture, and how it relates to other cultures. CQ is imperative for your ability to engage successfully in any business endeavor or social environment.

Culture is the way we make sense of the world and how we view it. It is a particular combination of values that drive specific forms of behavior.

Culture Shock is when *expectations* and the *reality* of the experience do not meet.

Deductive speech is presenting the background first (history, methodology, context, etc), and proceeds in the direction of the conclusion.

DIE is tool designed to help one slow down the knee-jerk reaction to jump to interpretation, and to make clear three pieces of data: Description, Interpretation, Expectation.

Direct is the focus of speech being concise and precise.

Doing-orientation is the preference of keeping busy during "down" time.

Emotional Intelligence (EQ) is the ability to identify, assess, and manage the intrapersonal, interpersonal, and group emotional dynamics.

Equality is the preference of treating others at *your* level, despite differences in gender, race, religion, age, weight, title, education, sexual orientation, marital status, number of children, dress, or socio-economic status.

Equifinality is the concept that there is not just one way to achieve your goals.

ESL is the acronym for English as a Second Language.

Ethnocentrism means the belief that one particular culture is the "right" one. To break the word down, "ethno" is "ethnicity," "centr" is the focus on the center, and "ism" is the "practice."

Expatriate is one who leaves his/her own country to work on a prolonged international assignment for his/her corporation in another country.

Explicit Culture includes the aspects of culture that you can *see* (tangible items) or *hear* (music, sounds, and words).

Expressive is the preference of releasing emotion in gestures and voice. All emotions are considered healthy.

Face Saving is a technique used by cultures where indirect communication is employed.

Fate is the preference of the environment to shape how each day, week, or quarter is played out.

Fixed Time is the preference to keep a schedule punctual.

Flatliners are people who are so angry at their situation that they feel comfort in being with others who they perceive as being in a similar situation and tend to congregate with them.

Fluid Time is the preference to keep a schedule that allows the individual to enjoy the moment.

Formal is the preference of a traditional nature in dress, language, behavior, and posture.

Generalizations make use of qualifiers to avoid the oversimplification of stereotypes.

Generation X is one born on and/or between the years of 1965 – 1980.

Group/Collectivism is the focus on whichever social circles to which you belong (e.g. families, organizations, alumni groups, etc.).

Groupthink is when the members of a group exhibit a type of common thought that develops into behavior/speech and is delivered in a way to try to minimize conflict and reach consensus.

Haptics is communication through the use of bodily contact. Tactile.

Hierarchy is the preference of treating others at *their* level according to differences in gender, race, religion, age, weight, title, education, sexual orientation, marital status, number of children, dress, or socio-economic status.

High Context is the focus on not so much of what you say as it is on how you say it. The information is Implicit and Indirect, and yet expected to be understood.

Homeostasis is an internal, stable condition of a living organism.

Idealism is the focus on maximizing the objective at a cost to preserve the dream or the aesthetic appeal.

Implicit Culture includes at the base Values and Beliefs that rise towards the surface in the form of Assumptions before manifesting into Explicit Culture.

Indirect is the focus of speech being diplomatic and harmonizing.

Individualism is the focus of people on themselves (and, often, their nuclear family).

Inductive speech is presenting the conclusion first, and may entail more information.

Individual culture is who you are as a person, and how you differ or relate to those from your national culture or sub-culture.

Informal is the preference of a casual nature in dress, language, behavior, and posture.

Inpatriate is one who enters your country from another country to work legally for his/her corporation on an international assignment.

Instrumental-orientation is the preference of maintaining control of emotion in all gestures and voice.

Kicked Puppy Syndrome is a term created by the author to refer to the behavior of when someone projects his/her anger onto you, it is really a reaction to a trigger that has its origin(s) in the past. The psychological term is *transference*.

Kinesics is communication through body movements, including facial expression, gestures, and posture.

Kinesthetic learner is one who learns best by touching and being "hands-on."

Ladder of Inference is a model used to illustrate that after we make an observation, we climb up towards assumptions and meaning, using our subjective experience to decide on an action or lack of action.

Low Context is the focus on words to convey meaning. The information is explicit and direct.

Mainstream culture is the culture that exerts the most influence over the regional occupants.

Materialism-orientation is the preference of acquiring possessions and placing more value on material objects than personal fulfillment attained intrinsically, without objects.

Mediation is a form of indirect communication that is practiced when a third person is used as a go-between.

Metamessage is the message conveyed between the lines or words.

Millennial is one born on and/or between the years of 1981 – 1999.

Monochronic is the cultural preference to handle one task or stream of communication at a time.

Monoglot/Monolingual is one who speaks but one language. Most Europeans joke the definition is "American."

Need for Certainty (Risk-Averse) -orientation is the preference to not move forward with any decisions until all of the information has been discussed at length.

NIMBY is the Political Science acronym used to represent "Not in My Back Yard." It refers to those who are interested in politics/news that pertain to their immediate geographical area. Local; not global.

Norms are unwritten rules of behavior that guide what members of small groups ought to do and not do.

Oculesics is communication through eye contact and gaze.

Organizational Architecture typically consists of Strategy, Structure, Process(es), Reward Systems, and People (Human Resource Management).

Organizational Culture is a pattern of assumptions, values, and norms that are shared by organization members.

Othello's Error is committed when one is predisposed to see a situation a certain way, thus leading to misinterpretation and false evaluation.

Outlier is a statistical term used to represent an observation that is numerically distant from the rest of the data. Anomaly. Aberration.

Pareto Principle (80-20 Rule) states that 80% of what happens is the result of 20% of the causes.

Particularism is making personal exceptions for a specific few.

Past-orientation is the focus on the past as a basis of making decisions in the present and for planning the future.

Peripheral Norms are norms easier to change because of their lower intensity. As they are of lesser importance to the group, they are thus easier to violate.

Pivotal Norms are those norms that the group pinpoints as critical to its survival. Given such importance, they are harder to change.

Polychronic is the cultural preference to handle multiple tasks or streams of communication concurrently.

Polyglot is one who speaks more than two languages.

Practical-orientation is the focus on maximizing the objective at the lowest financial cost, time-associated cost, and risk.

Present-Future Orientation is the preference of only considering what is pertinent in the moment and the immediate future.

Private Space is the preference of keeping an amplified personal bubble.

Process-oriented Learners prefer to acquire a lot of knowledge before they begin implementation. The focus is on quality.

Project Manager's Pyramid holds the premise that a manager can only have two of the following variables at any time, and the third variable must suffer: Quality (Q), Time (T), Cost ($).

Proxemics is communication through the use of space.

PTO is the acronym used for Paid Time Off.

Public Space is the preference for "intimate" proximity, meaning close-range.

Qualifiers are words such as "some," "many," "most" that define the quality of the statement and keep it from being a stereotype or an absolute statement.

Refraction is a form of indirect communication practiced when statements intended for one person are made to another, while that first person is present.

Relationship-orientation is the focus placed on maintaining and establishing strong social networks before tasks can be done.

Repatriate is one who left his/her country to work for his/her corporation overseas on an international assignment and has returned to the country of origin.

Reward Band includes those employees/people whose behavior receives recognition, bonuses, promotions, favoritism, etc.

ROW is an acronym used for "Rest of World." Not recommended. Stick with "International" and "Domestic."

Rule of 3 is to offer your guest something at least three times before accepting that they really mean "no."

Scotoma is when the mind blocks out the incongruity of the situation.

Scripts are imported when people have feelings that have been left unresolved.

Social Cognitive Theory maintains that the way you think and feel becomes altered, depending on with whom and where you socialize.

Spiritualism-orientation is the preference of finding intrinsic happiness. Usually, Spiritualists find peace in Nature.

Stereotype is one statement that is applied to every member of a particular culture.

Sub-cultures are all of the other cultures that exist in the region of the mainstream culture.

Sustained Competitive Advantage is attained if the organization is valuable, rare, and imperfectly inimitable.

Taboo Subjects of conversation are those topics that are not spoken about openly.

Tactile learner is the same as Kinesthetic Learner – one who learns best by touching or being "hands-on."

Task-orientation is when the focus is placed on the task you wish to accomplish.

Task-oriented learners are comfortable with trial and error. The focus is on momentum and quantity.

Tolerance for Ambiguity (Risk-Takers)-orientation is the preference to continue or move forward with a decision despite not having all of the information.

Traditionalist is one who is born on and/or between the years of 1901 – 1945.

Tradition-orientation is the preference to maintain whatever processes are in place because they work and/or are comfortable.

Transition is internal. It is the psychological process we go through in order to come to terms with a new situation.

Triumvirate of Hierarchy is a term used to describe a culture that definitively and unequivocally holds the value of Hierarchy by nature of three factors: Military History, Catholicism; Monarchy. Note that Spain is an exception that has evolved from its past.

Universalism is applying one rule to all.

Visual Learner is one who learns best by seeing or visualizing material and/or data.

REFERENCES

About, Inc. 2006. Human Resource Poll Results. Retrieved May 1, 2006, from http://humanresources.about.com/gi/pages/poll.htm?linkbac k.

Administaff. 2007. *"Generations in the Workplace: Changing at Warp Speed."*

Barney, Jay. 1986. *"Organizational Culture: Can it be a Source of Sustained Competitive Advantage?"* Academy of Management Review Journal.

Beamer, Linda & Varner, Iris. 1995. *Intercultural Communication in the Global Workplace*. New York: Irwin/McGraw-Hill.

Beckhard, Richard & Harris, Reuben T. 1987. *Organizational Transitions: Managing Complex Change*. Reading, Massachusetts: Addison-Wesley.

Bibikova, A. & Kotelnikov, V. *Cultural Intelligence (CQ)*. Retrieved May 1, 2006, from http:/www.1000ventures.com/business_guide/crosscuttings/c ultural_intelligence.html.

Biech, Elaine. 2005. *Training for Dummies*. Indianapolis, Indiana: Wiley Publishing.

Block, Peter. 2008. *Community*. San Francisco, California: Berrett-Koehler Publishers, Inc.

Boyatzis, R. 1982. *The Competent Manager: A Model for Effective Performance*. New York, New York: John Wiley and Sons.

Bradford, David L. & Burke, W. Warner. 2005. *Reinventing Organization Development*. San Francisco, California: Pfeiffer.

Bridges, William. 1991. *Managing Transitions; Making the Most of Change*. Philadelphia, Pennsylvania: Da Capo Press Books.

Cameron, Kim S. & Quinn, Robert E. 2005. *Diagnosing and Changing Organizational Culture: Based on the Competing Values Framework* (The Jossey-Bass Business & Management Series). San Francisco, California: Jossey-Bass.

Caruso, David R. & Salovey, Peter. 2004. *The Emotionally Intelligent Manager: How to Develop and Use the Four Key Emotional Skills of Leadership*. San Francisco, California: Jossey-Bass.

Cavallo, Kathleen, PsyD. 2004. *"Emotional Competence and Leadership Excellence at Johnson & Johnson: The Emotional Intelligence and Leadership Study."* Retrieved May 1, 2006, http://www.eiconsortium.org/research/jj_ei_study.htm

Cherniss, Cary, Ph.D. 2004. *"The Business Case for Emotional Intelligence."* Retrieved May 1, 2006, from http://eiconsortium.org/research/business_case_for_ei.htm

Cherniss, Cary & Adler, Mitchel. 2000. *Promoting Emotional Intelligence in Organizations*. Alexandria, Virginia: American Society for Training and Development.

Clapp, Neale W. 1974. *"Work Group Norms: Leverage for Organizational Change."* Ohio: Block Petrella Associates.

Combiendebises.free.fr

Cooper, Evan. 2000. *"Job Stickiness."* Retrieved May 1, 2006, http://www.morebusiness.com/running_your_business/mana gement/ d952374028.brc

Cooperrider, David L. & Whitney, Diana. 2005. *Appreciative Inquiry*. San Francisco, California: Berrett-Koehler Publishers, Inc.

Cornelius Grove & Associates, LLC. 2000. Gateway to the USA. Brooklyn, New York.

Coupland, Douglas. 1991. *Generation X: Tales for an Accelerated Culture*. New York City, New York: St. Martin's Press.

Cummings, Thomas G. & Worley, Christopher G. 1997. *Organization Development and Change*. Cincinnati, OH: West Publishing Company.

Damasio, A. 1994. *Descartes' Error: Emotion, Reason, and the Human Brain*. New York, New York: Grosset/Putnam.

Ekman, Paul 2003. *Emotions Revealed*. New York: Owl Books.

Emmerling, Robert, Psy.D. 2004. Emotional Competence Framework. Retrieved May 1, 2006, from http://www.eiconsortium.org/research/emotional_competence_framework

Francesco, Anne Marie & Gold, Barry Allen. 1998. *International Organizational Behavior*. Upper Saddle River, New Jersey: Prentice Hall.

Gallup Survey. 2007. Results on Quality Workplaces. Retrieved May 9, 2007, http://www.octanner.com/news/Gallup_Survey.htm.

Gittell, Jody Hoffer Ph.D. 2003. *The Southwest Airlines Way: Using the Power of Relationships to Achieve High Performance*. New York, New York:McGraw-Hill Companies.

Gladwell, Malcolm. 2008. *Outliers*. New York: New York. Back Bay Books. Pp.216-217.

Goleman, Daniel, Boyatzis, Richard E. & McKee, Annie. 2004. *Primal Leadership: Learning to Lead with Emotional Intelligence*.

Goleman, Daniel. 2000. *The Emotionally Intelligent Workplace*. New York, New York: Bantam Books.

Goleman, Daniel. 1998. *Working with Emotional Intelligence*. New York, New York: Bantam Books.

Grimme, Don. 2006. Grimme's *"Top Ten Tips to Attract, Retain and Motivate Employee."* Retrieved May 1, 2006, from http://www.speaking.com/articles_html/DonGrimme_889.html.

Heathfield, Susan M. 2006. *"Why Retention?"* Retrieved May 1, 2006, http://humanresources.about.com/od/retention/a/more_rete ntion.htm

Hofstede, Geert. 1997. *Cultures and Organizations: Software of the Mind*. New York: McGraw-Hill International.

Intel. 2004. *"Measuring Employee Productivity: Data Collection and Analysis Methods for Productivity Studies at Intel."* Retrieved May 1, 2006, from http://www.intel.com/it/business-management/employee-productivity.html

IOR. 2007. Global Solution Series. Working Effectively with China. Session #2.

Janis, Irving L. 1972. *Victims of Groupthink*. Boston: Houghton Mifflin Company.

Kaplan, Robert S. and Norton, David P. 2001. *The Strategy-Focused Organization*. Boston, Massachusetts: Harvard Business School Press.

Katzenbach, Jon R. & Smith, Douglas K. 2003. *The Wisdom of Teams: Creating the High-Performance Organization*. McKinsey & Company. Boston, Massachusetts: Harvard Business School Press.

Kohls, Robert L. & Knight, John N. 1994. *Developing Intercultural Awareness: A Cross-Cultural Training Handbook*. Yarmouth: Maine. Intercultural Press, Inc.

Lawler, Edward E. III and Worley, Christopher G. 2006. *Built to Change*. San Francisco: Jossey-Bass.

Patten, Mildred L. 2002. *Understanding Research Methods*. (3rd Edition). Los Angeles: Pyrczak Publishing.

Peninusla, The. *"Wife for vacation: Qataris marry poor women just for the holidays!"* Web posted at: 8/6/2006 3:26:20. www.thepeninsulaqatar.com.

Pollock, David C. Van Reken, Ruth E. Third Culture Kids: Growing Up Among Worlds. 2009. Boston: Nicholas Brealey Publishing.

Pricewaterhouse Coopers and Cranfield University School of Management UK. 2007. *"Relocation Trends: Measuring the Value of International Assignments."* Retrieved March 15, 2007, from http://www.vedior.com/vedior-hr-portal/english-articles-folder/measuring-the-value-of-international-assignments.html.

Prudential Resources Management. 1997. *Repatriation*. New York.

Schein, Edgar H. (1992). *Organizational Culture and Leadership*. 2nd edition. Reading, Massachusetts: Addison-Wesley.

Seddon, Mike. (2006). "Can Listening to Music Help Us Work Better?" www.articlesbase.com, Posted: Oct 30th, 2006.

Sherwell, Philip. "A Quiet Word to Loud Americans." Sydney Morning Herald. April 17, 2006. Smh.com.au.

Thomas, Gordon. 2005. *Gideon's Spies.* New York: St. Martin's Press, pg. 63.

Trompenaars, Alfons. 1998 *Riding the Waves of Culture: Understanding Diversity in Global Business.* New York: McGraw-Hill. Pg. 35.

USA Today, February 24, 1010. Medals table, 1D.

Webster's Ninth New Collegiate Dictionary. 1991. Springfield, Massachusetts: Merriam-Webster, Inc.

Windham International. 1999. *Global Relocation Trends*. New York: New York. Windham International.

Wolfe, Edward R. 2006. *"Rate of Return."* Retrieved May 1, 2006, from http://www.en.wikipedia.org/wiki/Return_on_investment

World Health Organization. 2006. WHO Global Competency Model. Retrieved May 1, 2006, from http://www.who.int/employment/competencies/en

Zander, Benjamin & Zander, Rosamund Stone. 2002. *The Art of Possibility*. Boston, Massachusetts: Penguin Books, Ltd.

ACKNOWLEDGEMENTS

I would like to first thank my husband Eddie and my two wonderful boys Kiran and Conner, for their love and support during the months that I crafted this book.

I would also like to thank all of my clients who have written me, shared their stories with me, and the several who have become my friends. I have learned so much from you. Thank you!

Odd as it may seem, I extend a big thanks to the Angwin community, home of my alma mater, a Liberal Arts college known as Pacific Union College. This is my *other* hometown. Without Angwin, I may not have learned the spirit of community.

Domo arigato gozaimasu ("thank you very much" in Japanese) to the man I consider my mentor, Brian Szepkouski. He is a man who has the knowledge, experience, passion, and presentation skills to be the paragon of the cross-cultural consultant.

I wouldn't have had the majority of my expatriates (or inpatriates and repatriates) without the recognition of those companies in the cross-cultural industry. Thank you to Berlitz Cross-Cultural Consulting, in particular Lyn Hopkins. Thank you Prudential Intercultural, in particular Louis Lima and Beverly Zimmerman. Thank you Cornelius Grove & Associates, in particular Dr. Cornelius Grove and Willa Hallowell. Thank you to Shepell-Family Guidance International. Thank you to International Orientation Resources. Thank you to Cultural Awareness International. Thank you to Val Bath, a true friend and respected colleague.

Much appreciation goes to Laura Lee (a.k.a. the Fountain). Laura is an Organization Development practitioner who balances reasoning with her heart and intelligence.

Thank YOU for taking the time to read this!

ABOUT THE AUTHOR

Rossina Gil is a Global Leadership & Organization Development Practitioner.   She specializes in analyzing corporate cultures and facilitating the alignment of the organizational values.

A California native, Ms. Gil has lived in Denmark, Spain, and Colombia. She has coached and consulted senior executives for 20 years in over 100 companies in seven countries, in English and Spanish.

She is the founder of Corporate Looking Glass, LLC, a team of Executive Coaches and Interculturalists, based across the USA. You may visit her site at www.CorporateLookingGlass.com

She holds a Master of Arts in International Studies from Claremont Graduate University; and a Master of Science in Organization Development from Pepperdine University's Graziadio School of Business and Management. Her undergraduate Bachelor degrees were earned at Pacific Union College (Napa Valley, California). These degrees signify that she enjoys learning, can digest and retain information well, and will work hard to meet deadlines with high quality deliverables. (She does not consider herself an egghead).

Ms. Gil loves to work with people and ideas. She is often described as empathetic, insightful, calm, and good humored. In her spare time, she enjoys running, swimming, reading, and people-watching. She currently resides in Brentwood, Tennessee, with her husband, two sons, and rescue dog Woody.

Contact her directly at: rossina@corporatelookingglass.com

64696974R00131

Made in the USA
Lexington, KY
16 June 2017